ELS MASTERS LANGUAGE STUDIES

MODULE 1: SOCIOLOGY

M1

Pearson Education, 221 River Street, Hoboken, NJ 07030

Staff credits: The people who made up the *University Success Oral Communication, Transition Level* team, representing content creation, design, manufacturing, marketing, multimedia, project management, publishing, rights management, and testing, are Pietro Alongi, Rhea Banker, Stephanie Bullard, Tracey Cataldo, Sara Davila, Mindy DePalma, Dave Dickey, Warren Fischbach, Nancy Flaggman, Gosia Jaros-White, Niki Lee, Amy McCormick, Jennifer Raspiller, Paula Van Ells, and Joseph Vella.

Project supervision: Debbie Sistino

Contributing editors: Eleanor Barnes, Andrea Bryant, Nancy Matsunaga, and Leigh Stolle

Cover image: DrAfter123/Getty Images

Text and cover design: Yin Ling Wong

Video research: Constance Rylance

Video production: Kristine Stolakis

Text composition: MPS Limited

Library of Congress Cataloging-in-Publication Data

A catalog record for the print edition is available from the Library of Congress.

ISBN-10: 0-13-541085-1

ISBN-13: 978-0-13-541085-1

Printed in Canada

7 2024

SUBJECT MATTER EXPERTS

Marcelo Clerici-Arias teaches undergraduate courses at Stanford University's Department of Economics, from principles of microeconomics and macroeconomics to upper-level courses in computational economics, behavioral economics, and economic policy. He has researched innovative pedagogies used in economics and other social and natural sciences. His main research areas are game theory, computational economics, and teaching and learning. Professor Clerici-Arias is a popular speaker and presenter, has participated in NSF-sponsored projects, and has coedited an economics textbook.

Jonathan D. Greenberg is a lecturer in law at Stanford Law School; teaching fellow for the school's advanced degree program in International Economic Law, Business & Policy; and scholar-in-residence at the school's Gould Center for Conflict Resolution. He has published scholarly articles and chapters in a broad range of interdisciplinary journals and books.

Robert Pogue Harrison is a professor of French and Italian literature at Stanford University and author of six books, the most recent of which is *Juvenescence: A Cultural History of Our Age* (2014). He writes regularly for the *New York Review of Books* and hosts the radio podcast *Entitled Opinions*. He is a member of the American Academy of Arts and Sciences, and in 2014, he was knighted Chevalier of the French Republic.

Lynn Hildemann is a professor of civil and environmental engineering at Stanford University and currently is serving as department chair. She is an author of over 80 peer-reviewed publications. Her research areas include the sources and dispersion of airborne particulate matter in indoor environments and assessment of human exposure to air pollutants. She has served on advisory committees for the Bay Area Air Quality Management District and the California Air Resources Board and as an associate editor for *Environmental Science & Technology*.

Robert Siegel is a professor in the Department of Microbiology and Immunology at Stanford University. He holds secondary appointments in the Program in Human Biology, the Center for African Studies, and the Woods Institute for the Environment. He is the recipient of numerous teaching awards including Stanford's highest teaching accolade, the Walter Gores Award. Dr. Siegel's courses cover a wide range of topics including virology, infectious disease, and global health, as well as molecular biology, Darwin and evolution and island biogeography, and photography. He is an avid hiker, photographer, and dromomaniac.

SERIES EDITORS

Robyn Brinks Lockwood teaches courses in spoken and written English at Stanford University in the English for Foreign Students graduate program and is the program education coordinator of the American Language and Culture undergraduate summer program. She is an active member of the international TESOL organization, serves as chairperson of the Publishing Professional Council, and is a past chair of the Materials Writers Interest Section. She is a frequent presenter at TESOL regional and international conferences. She has edited and written numerous textbooks, online courses, and ancillary components for ESL courses and TOEFL preparation.

Maggie Sokolik holds a BA in anthropology from Reed College and an MA in romance linguistics and a PhD in applied linguistics from UCLA. She is the author of over 20 ESL and composition textbooks. She has taught at MIT, Harvard, Texas A&M, and currently UC Berkeley, where she is director of College Writing Programs. She has developed and taught several popular MOOC courses in English language writing and literature. She is the founding editor of *TESL-EJ*, a peer-reviewed journal for ESL/EFL professionals, one of the first online journals. She travels frequently to speak about grammar, writing, and instructor education. She lives in the San Francisco Bay area, where she and her husband play bluegrass music.

Lawrence J. Zwier is an associate director of the English Language Center, Michigan State University. He holds a bachelor's degree in English literature from Aquinas College, Grand Rapids, MI, and an MA in TESL from the University of Minnesota. He has taught ESL/EFL at universities in Saudi Arabia, Malaysia, Japan, Singapore, and the United States. He is the author of numerous ELT textbooks, mostly about reading and vocabulary, and also writes nonfiction books about history and geography for middle school and high school students. He is married with two children and lives in Okemos, Michigan.

Contents

Key Features vi
Scope and Sequence xi

PART 1: FUNDAMENTAL ORAL COMMUNICATION SKILLS

SOCIOLOGY: Active Participation 2

PART 2: CRITICAL THINKING SKILLS

SOCIOLOGY: Facts and Opinions 18

PART 3: EXTENDED LECTURES

SOCIOLOGY: Five Revolutions 42

Credits 49

Key Features

UNIQUE PART STRUCTURE

This book employs a unique three-part structure, providing maximum flexibility and multiple opportunities to customize the flow of content.

Each part is a self-contained module allowing teachers to focus on the highest value skills and content. Parts are aligned around science, technology, engineering, arts, and mathematic (STEAM) content relevant to mainstream academic areas of study.

Part 1 and Part 2 focus on the fundamental and critical thinking skills most relevant for students preparing for university degrees. **Part 3** introduces students to extended practice with the skills. Students work directly with the authentic content created and delivered by top professors in their academic fields.

PART 1 AND PART 2

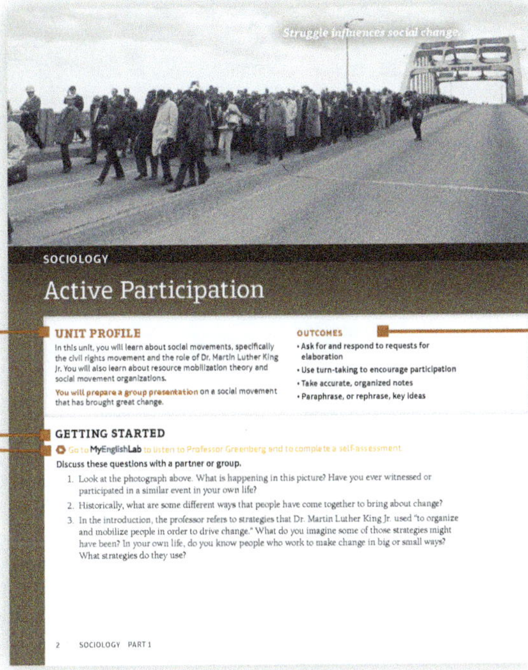
Struggle influences social change.

SOCIOLOGY

Active Participation

UNIT PROFILE

In this unit, you will learn about social movements, specifically the civil rights movement and the role of Dr. Martin Luther King Jr. You will also learn about resource mobilization theory and social movement organizations.

You will prepare a group presentation on a social movement that has brought great change.

OUTCOMES

- Ask for and respond to requests for elaboration
- Use turn-taking to encourage participation
- Take accurate, organized notes
- Paraphrase, or rephrase, key ideas

GETTING STARTED

Go to MyEnglishLab to listen to Professor Greenberg and to complete a self-assessment.

Discuss these questions with a partner or group.

1. Look at the photograph above. What is happening in this picture? Have you ever witnessed or participated in a similar event in your own life?
2. Historically, what are some different ways that people have come together to bring about change?
3. In the introduction, the professor refers to strategies that Dr. Martin Luther King Jr. used "to organize and mobilize people in order to drive change." What do you imagine some of those strategies might have been? In your own life, do you know people who work to make change in big or small ways? What strategies do they use?

2 SOCIOLOGY PART 1

A **Unit Profile** outlines the content.

Getting started questions explore the content, develop context, and engage students' prior knowledge.

An **online self-assessment** identifies skill areas for improvement and helps students create personal learning objectives.

Outcomes aligned with the Global Scale of English (GSE) are clearly stated to ensure student awareness of skills.

Professors provide a **preview** and a **summary** of the content.

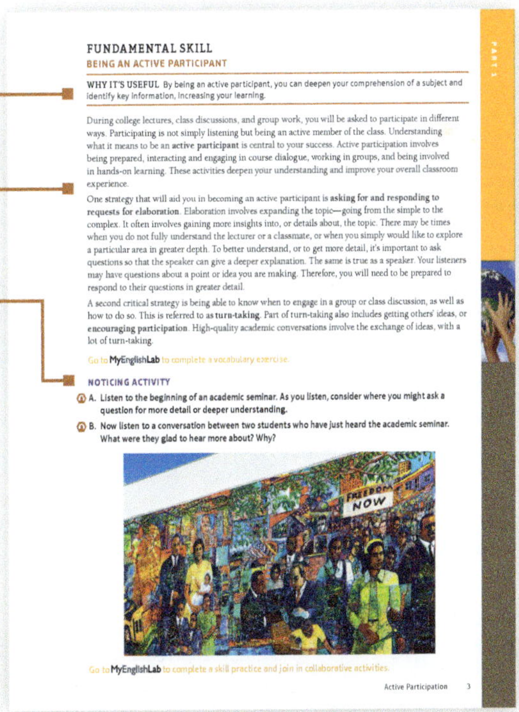
PART 1

FUNDAMENTAL SKILL

BEING AN ACTIVE PARTICIPANT

WHY IT'S USEFUL By being an active participant, you can deepen your comprehension of a subject and identify key information, increasing your learning.

During college lectures, class discussions, and group work, you will be asked to participate in different ways. Participating is not simply listening but being an active member of the class. Understanding what it means to be an **active participant** is central to your success. Active participation involves being prepared, interacting and engaging in course dialogue, working in groups, and being involved in hands-on learning. These activities deepen your understanding and improve your overall classroom experience.

One strategy that will aid you in becoming an active participant is **asking for and responding to requests for elaboration**. Elaboration involves expanding the topic—going from the simple to the complex. It often involves gaining more insights into, or details about, the topic. There may be times when you do not fully understand the lecturer or a classmate, or when you simply would like to explore a particular area in greater depth. To better understand, or to get more detail, it's important to ask questions so that the speaker can give a deeper explanation. The same is true as a speaker. Your listeners may have questions about a point or idea you are making. Therefore, you will need to be prepared to respond to their questions in greater detail.

A second critical strategy is being able to know when to engage in a group or class discussion, as well as how to do so. This is referred to as **turn-taking**. Part of turn-taking also includes getting others' ideas, or **encouraging participation**. High-quality academic conversations involve the exchange of ideas, with a lot of turn-taking.

Go to MyEnglishLab to complete a vocabulary exercise.

NOTICING ACTIVITY

A. Listen to the beginning of an academic seminar. As you listen, consider where you might ask a question for more detail or deeper understanding.

B. Now listen to a conversation between two students who have just heard the academic seminar. What were they glad to hear more about? Why?

Go to MyEnglishLab to complete a skill practice and join in collaborative activities.

Active Participation 3

Why It's Useful highlights the purpose for developing skills and supports transfer of skills to mainstream class content.

A **detailed presentation** contextualizes the skills value in academic study.

Noticing activities allow students to see skills demonstrated in the contexts of academic lectures, discussions, and question and answer sessions.

Each skill is divided into discreet **supporting skill** areas.

Multiple **exercises** encourage application of the skills and build fundamental and critical thinking skills.

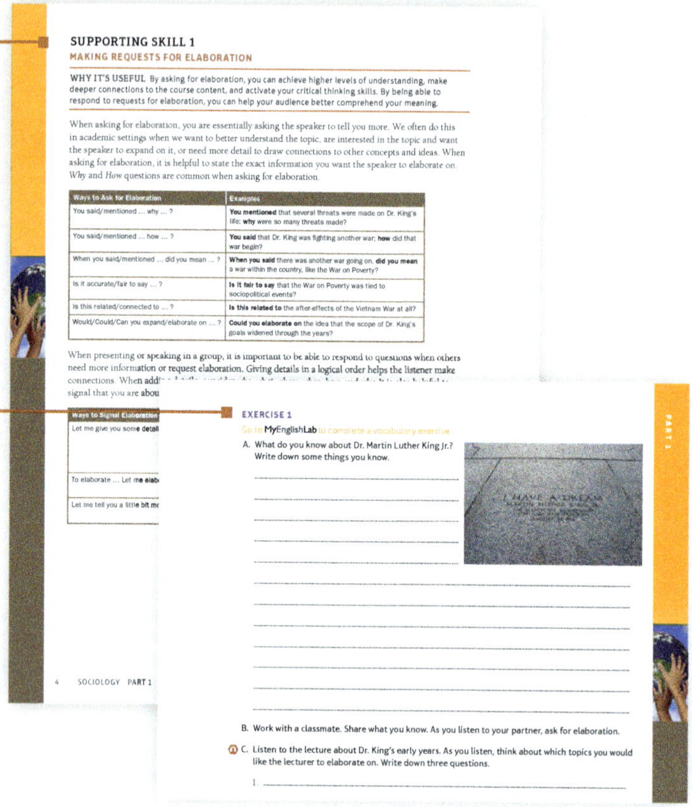

SUPPORTING SKILL 1

MAKING REQUESTS FOR ELABORATION

WHY IT'S USEFUL By asking for elaboration, you can achieve higher levels of understanding, make deeper connections to the course content, and activate your critical thinking skills. By being able to respond to requests for elaboration, you can help your audience better comprehend your meaning.

When asking for elaboration, you are essentially asking the speaker to tell you more. We often do this in academic settings when we want to better understand the topic, are interested in the topic and want the speaker to expand on it, or need more detail to draw connections to other concepts and ideas. When asking for elaboration, it is helpful to state the exact information you want the speaker to elaborate on. *Why* and *How* questions are common when asking for elaboration.

Ways to Ask for Elaboration	Examples
You said/mentioned ... why ... ?	**You mentioned** that several threats were made on Dr. King's life; **why** were so many threats made?
You said/mentioned ... how ... ?	**You said** that Dr. King was fighting another war; **how** did that war begin?
When you said/mentioned ... did you mean ... ?	**When you said** there was another war going on, **did you mean** a war within the country, like the War on Poverty?
Is it accurate/fair to say ... ?	**Is it fair to say** that the War on Poverty was tied to sociopolitical events?
Is this related/connected to ... ?	**Is this related to** the after-effects of the Vietnam War at all?
Would/Could/Can you expand/elaborate on ... ?	**Could you elaborate on** the idea that the scope of Dr. King's goals widened through the years?

When presenting or speaking in a group, it is important to be able to respond to questions when others need more information or request elaboration. Giving details in a logical order helps the listener make connections. When add...

signal that you are abou...

Ways to Signal Elaboration
Let me give you some detail...
To elaborate ... Let me elab...
Let me tell you a little bit m...

4 SOCIOLOGY PART 1

EXERCISE 1

Go to **MyEnglishLab** to complete a vocabulary exercise.

A. What do you know about Dr. Martin Luther King Jr.? Write down some things you know.

B. Work with a classmate. Share what you know. As you listen to your partner, ask for elaboration.

C. Listen to the lecture about Dr. King's early years. As you listen, think about which topics you would like the lecturer to elaborate on. Write down three questions.

1.

PART 1

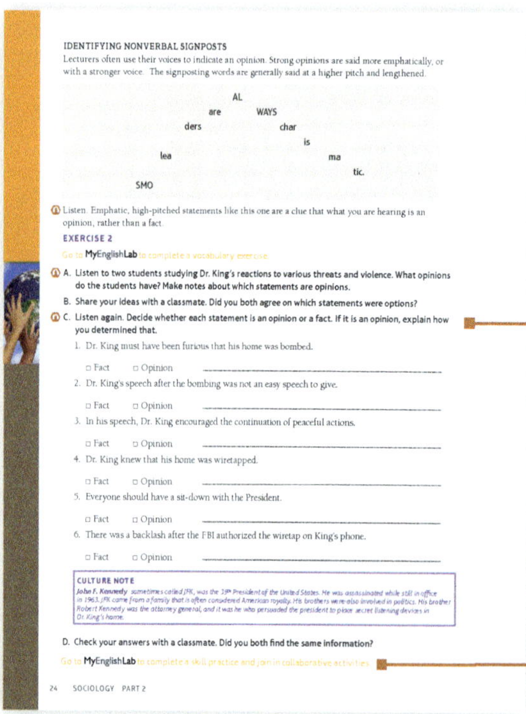

IDENTIFYING NONVERBAL SIGNPOSTS

Lecturers often use their voices to indicate an opinion. Strong opinions are said more emphatically, or with a stronger voice. The signposting words are generally said at a higher pitch and lengthened.

AL
are WAYS
ders char
is
lea ma
tic.
SMO

Listen. Emphatic, high-pitched statements like this one are a clue that what you are hearing is an opinion, rather than a fact.

EXERCISE 2

Go to **MyEnglishLab** to complete a vocabulary exercise.

A. Listen to two students studying Dr. King's reactions to various threats and violence. What opinions do the students have? Make notes about which statements are opinions.

B. Share your ideas with a classmate. Did you both agree on which statements were options?

C. Listen again. Decide whether each statement is an opinion or a fact. If it is an opinion, explain how you determined that.

1. Dr. King must have been furious that his home was bombed.
   □ Fact □ Opinion ____________
2. Dr. King's speech after the bombing was not an easy speech to give.
   □ Fact □ Opinion ____________
3. In his speech, Dr. King encouraged the continuation of peaceful actions.
   □ Fact □ Opinion ____________
4. Dr. King knew that his home was wiretapped.
   □ Fact □ Opinion ____________
5. Everyone should have a sit-down with the President.
   □ Fact □ Opinion ____________
6. There was a backlash after the FBI authorized the wiretap on King's phone.
   □ Fact □ Opinion ____________

CULTURE NOTE

John F. Kennedy sometimes called JFK, was the 35th President of the United States. He was assassinated while still in office in 1963. JFK came from a family that is often considered American royalty. His brothers were also involved in politics. His brother Robert Kennedy was the attorney general, and it was he who persuaded the president to place secret listening devices in Dr. King's home.

D. Check your answers with a classmate. Did you both find the same information?

Go to **MyEnglishLab** to complete a skill practice and join in collaborative activities.

24 SOCIOLOGY PART 2

A variety of listening types including lectures and academic discussions represent "real-life" university experiences.

Online activities encourage students to personalize content with collaborative research activities.

Integrated skills provide practice with high-level authentic academic content relevant to mainstream study.

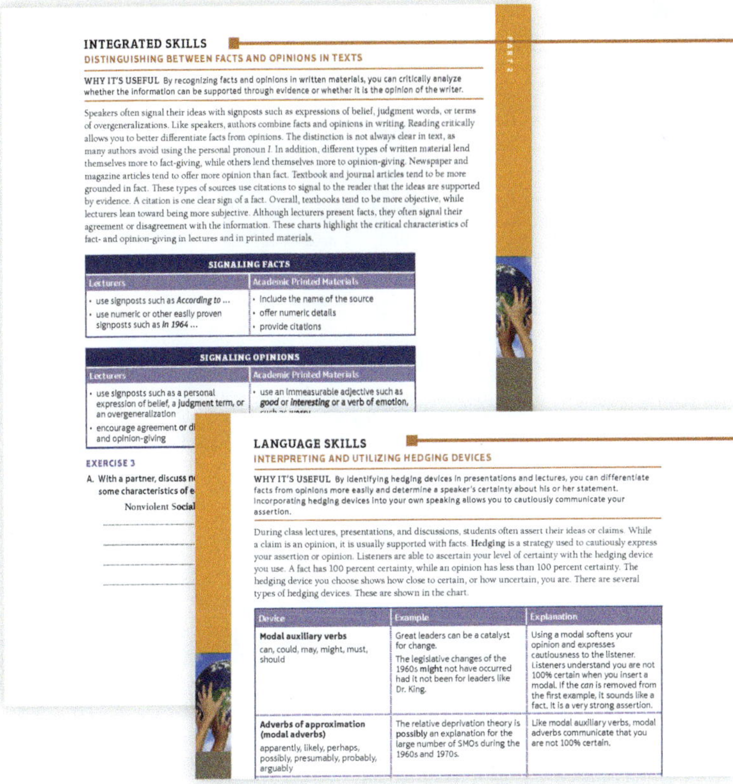

INTEGRATED SKILLS

DISTINGUISHING BETWEEN FACTS AND OPINIONS IN TEXTS

WHY IT'S USEFUL By recognizing facts and opinions in written materials, you can critically analyze whether the information can be supported through evidence or whether it is the opinion of the writer.

Speakers often signal their ideas with signposts such as expressions of belief, judgment words, or terms of overgeneralizations. Like speakers, authors combine facts and opinions in writing. Reading critically allows you to better differentiate facts from opinions. The distinction is not always clear in text, as many authors avoid using the personal pronoun *I*. In addition, different types of written material lend themselves more to fact-giving, while others lend themselves more to opinion-giving. Newspaper and magazine articles tend to offer more opinion than fact. Textbook and journal articles tend to be more grounded in fact. These types of sources use citations to signal to the reader that the ideas are supported by evidence. A citation is one clear sign of a fact. Overall, textbooks tend to be more objective, while lecturers lean toward being more subjective. Although lecturers present facts, they often signal their agreement or disagreement with the information. These charts highlight the critical characteristics of fact- and opinion-giving in lectures and in printed materials.

SIGNALING FACTS	
Lecturers	Academic Printed Materials
• use signposts such as *According to …* • use numeric or other easily proven signposts such as *In 1964 …*	• include the name of the source • offer numeric details • provide citations

SIGNALING OPINIONS	
Lecturers	Academic Printed Materials
• use signposts such as a personal expression of belief, a judgment term, or an overgeneralization • encourage agreement or di… and opinion-giving	• use an immeasurable adjective such as *good* or *interesting* or a verb of emotion, …

EXERCISE 3

A. With a partner, discuss … some characteristics of e…

Nonviolent Social…

LANGUAGE SKILLS

INTERPRETING AND UTILIZING HEDGING DEVICES

WHY IT'S USEFUL By identifying hedging devices in presentations and lectures, you can differentiate facts from opinions more easily and determine a speaker's certainty about his or her statement. Incorporating hedging devices into your own speaking allows you to cautiously communicate your assertion.

During class lectures, presentations, and discussions, students often assert their ideas or claims. While a claim is an opinion, it is usually supported with facts. **Hedging** is a strategy used to cautiously express your assertion or opinion. Listeners are able to ascertain your level of certainty with the hedging device you use. A fact has 100 percent certainty, while an opinion has less than 100 percent certainty. The hedging device you choose shows how close to certain, or how uncertain, you are. There are several types of hedging devices. These are shown in the chart.

Device	Example	Explanation
Modal auxiliary verbs can, could, may, might, must, should	Great leaders can be a catalyst for change. The legislative changes of the 1960s **might** not have occurred had it not been for leaders like Dr. King.	Using a modal softens your opinion and expresses cautiousness to the listener. Listeners understand you are not 100% certain when you insert a modal. If the *can* is removed from the first example, it sounds like a fact. It is a very strong assertion.
Adverbs of approximation (modal adverbs) apparently, likely, perhaps, possibly, presumably, probably, arguably	The relative deprivation theory is **possibly** an explanation for the large number of SMOs during the 1960s and 1970s.	Like modal auxiliary verbs, modal adverbs communicate that you are not 100% certain.

Language skill study provides support for complex lexical and grammatical skills.

A **lecture** aligned with the academic content allows students to apply skills practiced in the unit. Critical thinking and visual thinking activities challenge students to dig deeper.

A **final project** allows students to integrate content and utilize all aspects of their oral communication skills. Projects include presentations, debates, and panel discussions.

Parts 1 and 2 end with an extended **application of skills** that functions as a formative assessment.

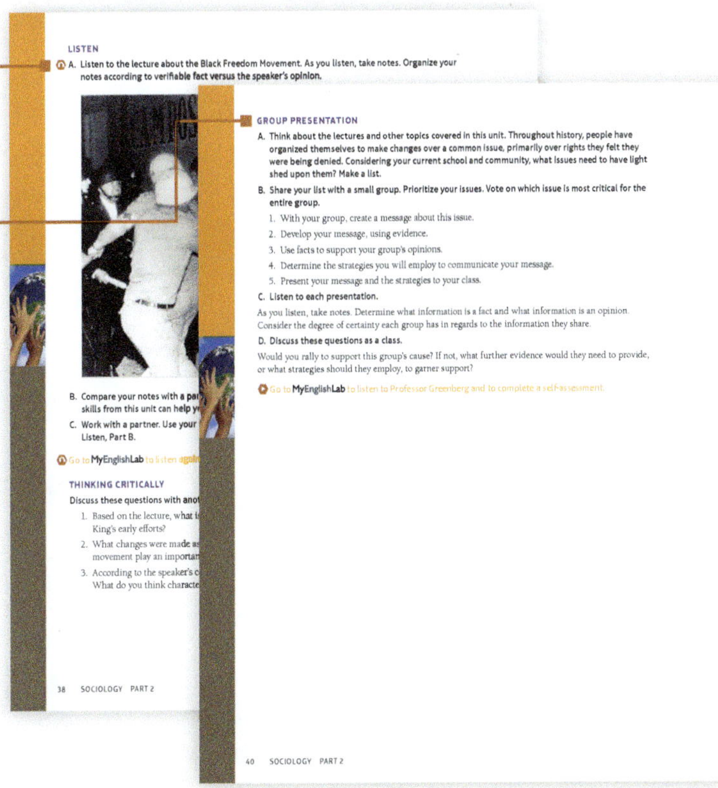

LISTEN

A. Listen to the lecture about the Black Freedom Movement. As you listen, take notes. Organize your notes according to verifiable fact versus the speaker's opinion.

B. Compare your notes with a par… skills from this unit can help y…

C. Work with a partner. Use your … Listen, Part B.

Go to MyEnglishLab to listen again…

THINKING CRITICALLY

Discuss these questions with ano…

1. Based on the lecture, what i… King's early efforts?
2. What changes were made a… movement play an importan…
3. According to the speaker's c… What do you think characte…

38 SOCIOLOGY PART 2

GROUP PRESENTATION

A. Think about the lectures and other topics covered in this unit. Throughout history, people have organized themselves to make changes over a common issue, primarily over rights they felt they were being denied. Considering your current school and community, what issues need to have light shed upon them? Make a list.

B. Share your list with a small group. Prioritize your issues. Vote on which issue is most critical for the entire group.

1. With your group, create a message about this issue.
2. Develop your message, using evidence.
3. Use facts to support your group's opinions.
4. Determine the strategies you will employ to communicate your message.
5. Present your message and the strategies to your class.

C. Listen to each presentation.

As you listen, take notes. Determine what information is a fact and what information is an opinion. Consider the degree of certainty each group has in regards to the information they share.

D. Discuss these questions as a class.

Would you rally to support this group's cause? If not, what further evidence would they need to provide, or what strategies should they employ, to garner support?

Go to MyEnglishLab to listen to Professor Greenberg and to complete a self-assessment.

40 SOCIOLOGY PART 2

PART 3

Critical thinking activities ask learners to engage at a deep level with the content, using information from the lecture to address specific real-world applications.

THINKING CRITICALLY

Consider each situation in light of what you heard in the lecture. By yourself or with a partner, apply what you know about nonviolent protest movements to address each situation.

Situation 1 In his lecture, Professor Greenberg describes how nonviolent actions were pivotal acts of revolution. In the 1960s, nonviolence had an impact on problems of racism, poverty, and militarism. Choose one of these problems and describe how nonviolent protest can bring attention to the situation and create long-lasting change.

Situation 2 Science and technology have had an extraordinary impact on the course of human history over the last fifty 50 years. These advances, however, have not come without consequences. Improvements in science and technology have been linked to overpopulation, global food shortages, and radical climate change. The same technology that provides solutions is fraught with challenges. Using strategies

Thinking visually provides an opportunity for students to create and analyze charts, graphs, and other visuals.

THINKING VISUALLY

A. Review the lecture, paying particular attention to important events and the years during which they occurred. Then create a timeline of 10 events mentioned by Professor Greenberg.

Students view an **authentic lecture** presented by a professor working in a specific STEAM field.

SOCIOLOGY

Five Revolutions

UNIT PROFILE

In this unit you will watch a lecture entitled "Five Revolutions." This lecture examines the peaceful revolutionary work of Dr. Martin Luther King Jr. and evaluates events that have influenced social change movements throughout North American history.

You will research a grassroots movement that has impacted people's lives in a positive way and prepare a short presentation on the movement.

EXTENDED LECTURE

BEFORE YOU VIEW

Think about these questions before watching the lecture "Five Revolutions." Discuss them with another student.

1. What is a revolution?
2. Why do you think people revolt? What are some of the reasons people organize together to revolt?

Language skills reviews language skills developed in Part 1 and Part 2, using the source content from the professor to provide final examples.

THINKING ABOUT LANGUAGE

PARAPHRASING

Paraphrase the boldface words in the sentences.

1. The essential **trope**, ____________ of Dr. King's National Cathedral homily is the cautionary tale of Rip Van Winkle.
2. The American Revolution also harnessed a tremendous **moral force**, ____________.
3. Usually the party that suffers the cruelty and **humiliation**, ____________.
4. Throughout the South, African Americans were **coerced**, ____________ into indentured servitude and forced labor by white plantation owners.
5. As a result, only a tiny **fraction**, ____________ of African Americans in 1955 were registered to vote.
6. Dr. Martin Luther King Jr. spoke about a triple revolution **unfolding**, ____________ in the present time.

HEDGING

Rewrite each assertive statement using a hedging device.

1. In life, too many people find themselves living amidst a great period of social change, and yet they fail to develop the new attitudes that the new situation demands.

____

____

2. The sole purpose of democratic government is to secure the rights of life, liberty, and the pursuit of happiness.

3. The compromise ma... colonies north and s...

4. The end of reconstru... to re-enslavement u...

5. Time after time Dr. ... national media, thus...

TIP

Hedging devices Speakers use hedging devices to soften, or more cautiously, assert their opinion. For common hedging devices, see SOCIOLOGY Part 2.

46 SOCIOLOGY PART 3

A **final collaborative activity** encourages in-class or online project collaboration, mirroring real-world expectations of project learning.

INDIVIDUAL PRESENTATION

The second revolution highlighted in the lecture began as a grassroots movement that spread across the country and the world to ignite a change. What are some other grassroots movements that have impacted people's lives? When and where did they begin? How did the message spread? How have people's lives been changed as a result?

Topic: Grassroots movement that has impacted people's lives in a positive way.

RESEARCH

A. Investigate other grassroots movements. Select a movement that interests you.

Grassroots movement ____________________

B. Research your grassroots movement by seeking out primary sources. Check that the materials you use and cite are from reputable and respected publications.

C. Prepare your presentation. Be sure to present your main ideas clearly and to support your ideas with evidence.

D. Practice presenting to a partner.

E. While listening to your partner, ask him or her to elaborate on ideas where you would like more information.

TIP

Elaborating on Ideas To explore a topic in greater depth, it is important to ask the speaker for more details about a particular point in order to receive a deeper explanation. For more information on elaboration, refer to SOCIOLOGY Part 1.

PRESENT

A. Listen to each class member's presentation. As you listen, complete the chart.

Movement	Time Period	Place	Key Leaders	Changes

Scope and Sequence

PART 1

Fundamental Oral Communication Skills is designed to build fundamental skills step by step through exploration of rigorous, academic content.

	FUNDAMENTAL SKILLS	SUPPORTING SKILLS	INTEGRATED SKILLS	LANGUAGE SKILLS	APPLY YOUR SKILLS
 SOCIOLOGY **Active Participation**	Be an active participant	• Make requests for elaboration • Use turn-taking to encourage participation	Take accurate, organized notes	Paraphrase key ideas	Prepare and deliver an informational group presentation on origins, evolution, and achievements of a social change movement

PART 2

Critical Thinking Skills moves from skill building to application of the skills that require critical thinking.

	CRITICAL THINKING SKILLS	SUPPORTING SKILLS	INTEGRATED SKILLS	LANGUAGE SKILLS	APPLY YOUR SKILLS
 SOCIOLOGY **Facts and Opinions**	Distinguish facts from opinions	• Identify facts through verbal and non-verbal signposts • Identify opinions through verbal and non-verbal signposts • Recognize and interpret statements of fact and opinion	Distinguish between facts and opinions in texts	Interpret and utilize hedging devices	Prepare and deliver a persuasive group presentation for an important change that needs to be made to a school or community

PART 3

Extended Lectures presents authentic content written and delivered by university professors. Academically rigorous application and assessment activities allow for a synthesis of the skills developed in Part 1 and Part 2.

	LECTURE	RESEARCH/ASSIGNMENT
 SOCIOLOGY	Five Revolutions	Research, prepare, and deliver an individual presentation on a grassroots social movement that has had an impact on society.

PART 1

Fundamental Oral Communication Skills

THE HUMAN EXPERIENCE
Sociology
ACTIVE PARTICIPATION 2

Part 1 is designed to build fundamental skills step by step through exploration of rigorous, academic content. Practice activities tied to specific learning outcomes in each unit focus on understanding the function and application of the skills.

SOCIOLOGY

Active Participation

UNIT PROFILE

In this unit, you will learn about social movements, specifically the civil rights movement and the role of Dr. Martin Luther King Jr. You will also learn about resource mobilization theory and social movement organizations.

You will prepare a group presentation on a social movement that has brought great change.

OUTCOMES

- Ask for and respond to requests for elaboration
- Use turn-taking to encourage participation
- Take accurate, organized notes
- Paraphrase, or rephrase, key ideas

GETTING STARTED

Go to MyEnglishLab to listen to Professor Greenberg and to complete a self-assessment.

Discuss these questions with a partner or group.

1. Look at the photograph above. What is happening in this picture? Have you ever witnessed or participated in a similar event in your own life?
2. Historically, what are some different ways that people have come together to bring about change?
3. In the introduction, the professor refers to strategies that Dr. Martin Luther King Jr. used "to organize and mobilize people in order to drive change." What do you imagine some of those strategies might have been? In your own life, do you know people who work to make change in big or small ways? What strategies do they use?

FUNDAMENTAL SKILL
BEING AN ACTIVE PARTICIPANT

WHY IT'S USEFUL By being an active participant, you can deepen your comprehension of a subject and identify key information, increasing your learning.

During college lectures, class discussions, and group work, you will be asked to participate in different ways. Participating is not simply listening but being an active member of the class. Understanding what it means to be an **active participant** is central to your success. Active participation involves being prepared, interacting and engaging in course dialogue, working in groups, and being involved in hands-on learning. These activities deepen your understanding and improve your overall classroom experience.

One strategy that will aid you in becoming an active participant is **asking for and responding to requests for elaboration**. Elaboration involves expanding the topic—going from the simple to the complex. It often involves gaining more insights into, or details about, the topic. There may be times when you do not fully understand the lecturer or a classmate, or when you simply would like to explore a particular area in greater depth. To better understand, or to get more detail, it's important to ask questions so that the speaker can give a deeper explanation. The same is true as a speaker. Your listeners may have questions about a point or idea you are making. Therefore, you will need to be prepared to respond to their questions in greater detail.

A second critical strategy is being able to know when to engage in a group or class discussion, as well as how to do so. This is referred to as **turn-taking**. Part of turn-taking also includes getting others' ideas, or **encouraging participation**. High-quality academic conversations involve the exchange of ideas, with a lot of turn-taking.

Go to MyEnglishLab to complete a vocabulary exercise.

NOTICING ACTIVITY

A. Listen to the beginning of an academic seminar. As you listen, consider where you might ask a question for more detail or deeper understanding.

B. Now listen to a conversation between two students who have just heard the academic seminar. What were they glad to hear more about? Why?

Go to MyEnglishLab to complete a skill practice and join in collaborative activities.

SUPPORTING SKILL 1

MAKING REQUESTS FOR ELABORATION

WHY IT'S USEFUL By asking for elaboration, you can achieve higher levels of understanding, make deeper connections to the course content, and activate your critical thinking skills. By being able to respond to requests for elaboration, you can help your audience better comprehend your meaning.

When asking for elaboration, you are essentially asking the speaker to tell you more. We often do this in academic settings when we want to better understand the topic, are interested in the topic and want the speaker to expand on it, or need more detail to draw connections to other concepts and ideas. When asking for elaboration, it is helpful to state the exact information you want the speaker to elaborate on. *Why* and *How* questions are common when asking for elaboration.

Ways to Ask for Elaboration	Examples
You said/mentioned ... why ... ?	**You mentioned** that several threats were made on Dr. King's life; **why** were so many threats made?
You said/mentioned ... how ... ?	**You said** that Dr. King was fighting another war; **how** did that war begin?
When you said/mentioned ... did you mean ... ?	**When you said** there was another war going on, **did you mean** a war within the country, like the War on Poverty?
Is it accurate/fair to say ... ?	**Is it fair to say** that the War on Poverty was tied to sociopolitical events?
Is this related/connected to ... ?	**Is this related to** the after-effects of the Vietnam War at all?
Would/Could/Can you expand/elaborate on ... ?	**Could you elaborate on** the idea that the scope of Dr. King's goals widened through the years?

When presenting or speaking in a group, it is important to be able to respond to questions when others need more information or request elaboration. Giving details in a logical order helps the listener make connections. When adding details, consider *who, what, where, when, how,* and *why.* It is also helpful to signal that you are about to elaborate.

Ways to Signal Elaboration	Examples
Let me give you some details. First ... Second ...	**Let me give you some details. First,** the sociopolitical climate was one in which the country was divided by race. **Second,** the political climate was also divided, as many Americans were against the war, while others deemed it necessary.
To elaborate ... Let me elaborate.	**Let me elaborate.** This took place in a very segregated town. Community members had literally drawn lines in the street.
Let me tell you a little bit more. What's more ...	**What's more is** Dr. King recruited the poor from the city and rural areas and led them in a campaign for fair wages.

EXERCISE 1

Go to MyEnglishLab to complete a vocabulary exercise.

A. What do you know about Dr. Martin Luther King Jr.? Write down some things you know.

....

....

....

....

....

....

....

....

....

....

....

....

B. Work with a classmate. Share what you know. As you listen to your partner, ask for elaboration.

C. Listen to the lecture about Dr. King's early years. As you listen, think about which topics you would like the lecturer to elaborate on. Write down three questions.

1. ....

2. ....

3. ....

D. In a small group, share your requests for elaboration. Choose two or three questions to ask your instructor.

Go to MyEnglishLab to complete a skill practice and join in collaborative activities.

SUPPORTING SKILL 2

TURN-TAKING AND ENCOURAGING PARTICIPATION

WHY IT'S USEFUL By identifying techniques used in spoken discourse for turn-taking and for encouraging participation, you can better understand and follow the unspoken regulations of organized academic discussions. By using these techniques when you speak, you can invite your listeners to actively engage in the topic with you.

Verbal interaction is a regular part of one's academic life. Understanding the unspoken rules for **turn-taking**, or when to enter or exit the conversation, is an important part of being an active participant.

ENTERING A CONVERSATION

You can enter the conversation when someone has finished his or her thought or idea. Some clues that the speaker has finished a thought are:

- a drop in intonation

  The college had few adult students, so it specifically opened up study to qualified younger students.

- a slower pace or lengthening of the last syllable

  His undergraduate degree was awarded by Morehouse College, a historically black college in At-lan-ta.

- a turn-taking signal, or cue

  ... you know.
  What do you think?
  That's my idea.
  Well ...
  Ah ...

Hearing one of these turn-taking techniques signals listeners that they may speak. When entering a conversation, speakers may begin:

Expressions Used for Entering a Conversation	Utterances Commonly Used before a Phrase
Can I add to that by saying ...	Well,
I'd like to say ...	Yes,
I'd like to add to that ...	So,
I'd like to give my two cents ...	But,
My idea is ...	Um,
One idea is ...	No/Nah,

Examples

Well, I'd like to give my two cents. *The political turmoil at the time definitely impacted the threats.*

So, my idea is *that many citizens chose not to engage and that also created problems.*

Um, *I'm not sure about that. I think they were fighting their own battles.*

EXITING A CONVERSATION

Turn-taking also involves giving up the floor, or allowing someone else to share his or her ideas. It is important to pay close attention to your listeners to determine if someone would like to ask a question, add to your ideas, or offer a new idea. Pay attention to:

- expressions
- body language (nodding in agreement or disagreement can indicate a listener has something to share)
- noises such as *uh-huh*, *hmmm*

ENCOURAGING PARTICIPATION

Lecturers often encourage listeners to participate and contribute ideas. This makes the class more dynamic and presents an opportunity for deeper learning. Lecturers may address you by name to ask you for your thoughts.

Example

How about you, Tiaxin?
What do you think, Ali?
Ming, can you add anything?
We haven't heard from you, Rosa.

Or, they may use an expression to encourage full participation.

Example

What does everyone think?
Any ideas or thoughts on that?
Does anyone want to add something here?

Go to MyEnglishLab to complete a vocabulary exercise.

EXERCISE 2

A. Read the discussion excerpt between a student and tutor and add expressions to encourage participation. Then role-play the conversation with a partner. Be sure to signal turn-taking with a drop in pitch and lengthened final syllables.

Tutor: Let's review social movements. ....

Student: Well, I think the professor defined social groups as large groups that don't have power, and they are trying to promote some sort of change in society.

Tutor: Yeah, and let's not forget that they are organized, unlike collective behaviors. As far as King and the civil rights movement, ...

Student: I think Dr. King's civil rights movement was definitely a social movement because it was organized, attempted to relieve tensions in society, and the group had legitimate expectations for change.

Tutor: Yes. So let's talk about social change. King led the movement to bring about change through his ability to lead the group. He knew how to reach people and mobilize them. ....

Student: Yes, I can add to that. He also was able to frame the group's message and advocate for them.

Tutor: I think you got it! You might be ready for the test.

B. Listen to the academic discussion. Choose all the signals of turn-taking and encouraging participation that you hear.

Turn-taking signals when finished speaking:

- □ lengthened syllables
- □ drop in pitch
- □ you know
- □ That's my idea.

Turn-taking signals when beginning to speak:

- □ I'll add to that by saying …
- □ I'd like to say …
- □ My idea is …
- □ Well,
- □ Nah,
- □ Um
- □ Yeah

Encouraging participation:

- □ How about you …?
- □ … what do you think?
- □ Any ideas?
- □ We haven't heard from you.
- □ Does anyone want to add something here?

C. Listen again and take notes on what you hear. With a partner, share what you remember from the excerpt. Practice using signals for turn-taking and encouraging participation.

Go to **MyEnglishLab** to complete a skill practice and join in collaborative activities.

INTEGRATED SKILLS

TAKING ACCURATE, ORGANIZED NOTES

WHY IT'S USEFUL By developing a systematic note-taking method, you can easily identify key points of a lecture, better understand the connections among related ideas, and have the needed tools to improve your overall performance on assignments and tests.

One of the greatest cognitive demands you have as a college student is taking notes during a lecture. Academic listening involves much more than just listening passively. You need to:

- select important ideas;
- interpret the information;
- determine what to write down and;
- record it in an organized manner.

The more accurate and organized your notes are, the more likely you are to be successful in your comprehension of the subject. Part of being an organized note taker is finding and utilizing a technique or method that works for you. You may find that one technique works better in one class, while a different method works in a different course. Common note-taking methods are:

- outlining
- the Cornell Method
- charting or mapping

OUTLINING

Outlining involves listening and writing key ideas based on space indentation. This makes it easy to identify the key ideas, supporting details, and examples. Information that is most general starts at the margin, while more specific details and examples are indented.

I. Civil Rights social movement
    A. Began in 1955 with Montgomery bus boycott
    B. Rosa Parks arrested for not surrendering her seat
        1. First lady of civil rights

THE CORNELL METHOD

The Cornell Method has two main parts: the first part you do in class, while listening, and the second part you do immediately after class. In class, you jot down notes on the right side of a paper. After class, you use the left side to pull out key ideas. This allows you to easily condense and identify key ideas within a lecture.

Social Movement Organization Leader: MLK Characteristics: 1. organize people 2. create/state message 3. exploit opportunities	MLK as a SMO leader Leaders have all kinds of characteristics. Organize people, frame a movement's message, exploit opportunities, gather people. These characteristics are important for leaders. They represent the collective group.

CHARTING OR MAPPING

Charting or mapping contains all key information and visually illustrates the relationships among ideas.

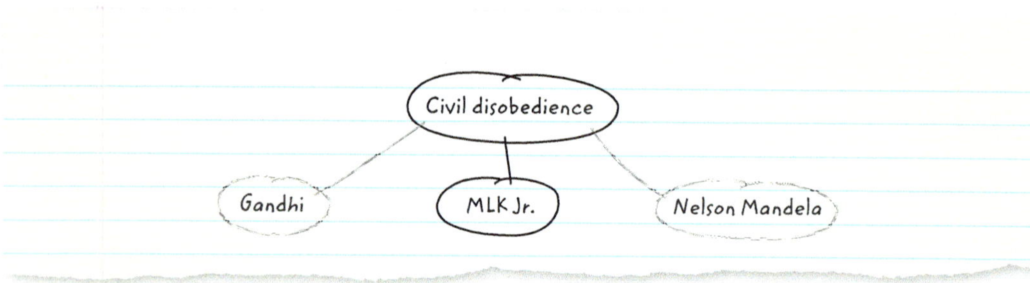

EXERCISE 3

A. **With a partner, review the three note-taking methods. What are the advantages and disadvantages of each method?**

B. **Now listen to a lecture on Dr. Martin Luther King's early adult life. Take notes using one of the methods.**

C. **Using your notes, answer the questions about the lecture.**

1. Can you number the events of Dr. King's life in chronological order?

   .... Dr. King's house bombed

   .... Married Coretta Scott

   .... Graduated from Morehouse College

   .... Earned PhD at Boston College

   .... Wrote "Letter from Birmingham Jail"

   .... Awarded Nobel Peace Prize

   .... Led march on Washington, DC to bring attention to civil rights

   .... Took leadership role after Montgomery bus boycott

   .... Gave famous "I Have a Dream" speech

   .... Assassinated in 1968

2. What were some results of Dr. King's efforts?
3. Why was Dr. King no longer the primary voice of the civil rights movement in 1964?
4. What are some other issues Dr. King spoke out against?

D. **With your partner, discuss which note-taking method you chose and why. Was it effective? Why or why not?**

Go to **MyEnglishLab** to complete a skill practice.

PART 1

LANGUAGE SKILL
PARAPHRASING KEY IDEAS

WHY IT'S USEFUL By identifying paraphrasing, you can determine the meaning of complex terms. You can also utilize paraphrasing techniques when speaking or presenting to clarify technical language for your listeners.

In academic lectures and discussions, discipline-specific language is often used. Lecturers often restate the meaning of these terms in a way that is easier for listeners to understand. This is referred to as **paraphrasing**, or rephrasing. For example, a lecturer might state:

"Dr. King's ascribed status, *or social position given by birth,* played a role in his desire to advocate."

The lecturer used the term *ascribed status,* followed by its definition. This is one common way lecturers paraphrase.

Language for Paraphrasing	Examples
By that I mean …	Dr. King had great discipline. **By that I mean** he was motivated to produce particular realities.
It's …	Remember when we discussed normalization? **It's** a social process by which some practices are marked as "normal," while others are marked as "abnormal."
In other words,	The ruling class ideology prevailed. **In other words**, those in charge promoted the idea that African Americans were different.
In a word,	King worked to lift the underclass—**in a word**, the poorest and most underprivileged.
Or	Dr. King's ascribed status, **or** social position given by birth, played a tremendous role in his desire to advocate.
That is to say,	Class conflicts, **that is to say**, the differences among the varying social classes, were also a concern of King's.
Use of appositive (definition)	The sanctions **(punishments)** put upon King did not slow his efforts.

EXERCISE 4

A. Look at the word list from this unit. Choose the words and phrases you know. If you don't remember the meaning, ask a classmate.

- □ boycott
- □ propel
- □ grassroots
- □ promised land
- □ shoulder the responsibility
- □ charisma
- □ segregate
- □ scrutinize
- □ passive resistance

B. Read the sentences, which include words and phrases from Part A. Add paraphrases of the terms where indicated.

1. Dr. King served as the primary spokesman for the bus boycott, ...
2. While the civil rights campaign began in the South, Dr. King propelled the movement, ... , to a national level.
3. The work of civil rights leaders was frequently scrutinized, ... , by others.
4. Although Dr. King was the face of the Civil Rights movement, it was truly a grassroots effort. ....
5. One critical leadership characteristic noted by sociologists is charisma. ....

C. Work with a partner. Make sentences using the words and phrases in Part A that are not used in Part B. Practice paraphrasing.

Go to MyEnglishLab to complete a skill practice.

APPLY YOUR SKILLS

WHY IT'S USEFUL By applying the skills you have learned in this unit, you will be able to more actively participate and engage in a college-level sociology lecture.

ASSIGNMENT

Prepare a group presentation on a social movement. Your group will present key elements of the movement, such as organizational support and mobilization, to explain how the movement started and gained momentum, as well as what changes it achieved.

BEFORE YOU LISTEN

A. Before you listen, discuss these questions with one or more students.

1. How do most grassroots efforts begin? How about the civil rights movement?
2. What is a boycott, and what do people boycott?
3. Why do you think Dr. King led a variety of boycotts?

B. You will listen to a lecture about the Montgomery bus boycott. As you listen to the lecture, think about these questions.

1. Why is Rosa Parks so well known for the Montgomery bus boycott?
2. What effect did her arrest have on the civil rights movement?
3. How was Dr. King involved?
4. What impact did the bus boycott have on the city of Montgomery?

C. Review the Unit Skills Summary. As you listen to the lecture and prepare for your group presentation, apply the skills you learned in this unit.

UNIT SKILLS SUMMARY

BE AN ACTIVE PARTICIPANT USING THESE SKILLS:

Utilize strategies for elaboration and turn-taking.

- Ask for and respond to questions to get and give more details.
- Use your voice and signposts to signal the end or beginning of your ideas.
- Identify when others want to take a turn.

Take accurate, organized notes.

- Utilize a method to help you systematically organize key ideas.
- Select, interpret, determine, and write down key ideas.

Paraphrase.

- Listen for restatements of key terms to determine meaning.
- Restate discipline-specific vocabulary to clarify technical language.

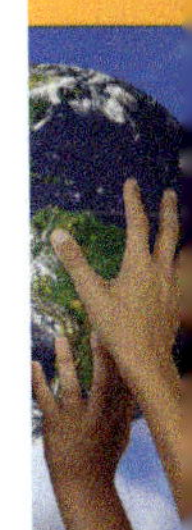

LISTEN

A. Listen to the lecture about the Montgomery bus boycott and take notes.

B. Compare your notes with a partner. Do you both have the same key ideas? What skills from this unit can help you identify key ideas?

C. Work with a partner. Use your notes on the listening to answer the questions from Before You Listen, Part B.

THINKING CRITICALLY

Discuss the questions with another student.

1. What do you think are the primary implications of the speaker's statement, "We remember Rosa Parks largely because, by the time of her arrest, the African American community of Montgomery, Alabama, had been ready and waiting for a 'test case' to oppose bus segregation laws"?
2. Based on the lecture, how would you describe the speaker's point of view? In your discussion, provide examples that illustrate your understanding.
3. Based on the lecture, do you think individuals can greatly influence social change? How?
4. What connection does the speaker suggest exists between everyday citizens and social change?

THINKING VISUALLY

A. Look at the bar graphs on this page and on the next page. Discuss these questions with a partner.

1. What are the most critical civil rights for the respondents?
2. Why do you think some people answered "Not at all important" to some categories?
3. Would your ranking of these issues be similar or different? How?
4. What other categories would you add to these?

HOW IMPORTANT ARE THESE CIVIL RIGHTS ISSUES TO YOU?

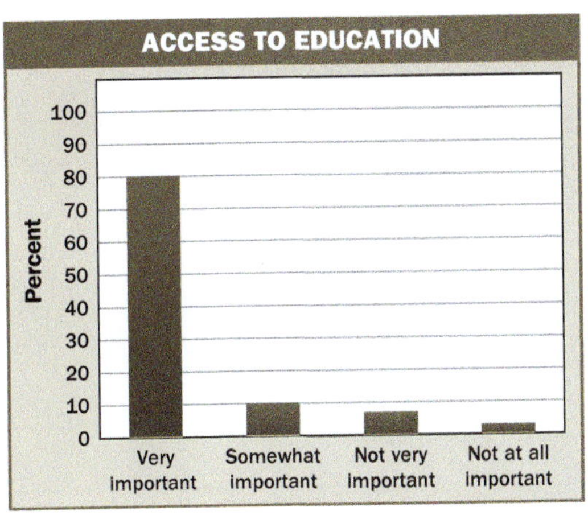

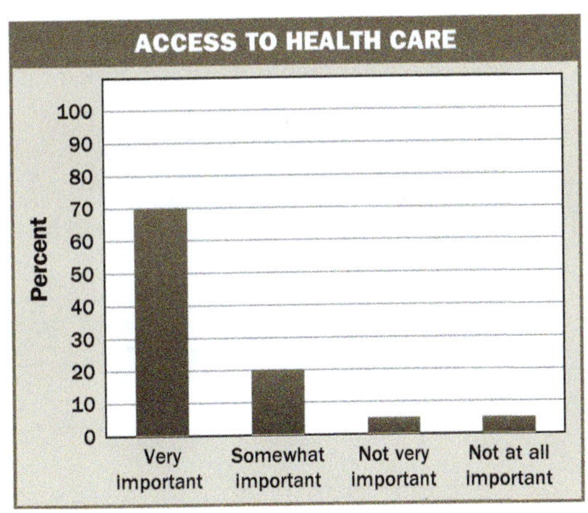

Continued

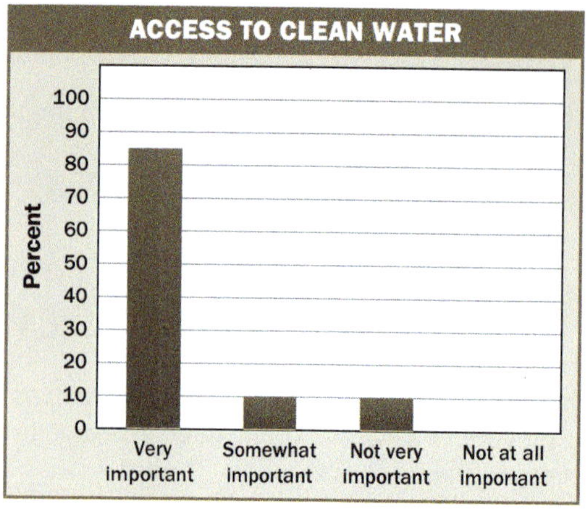

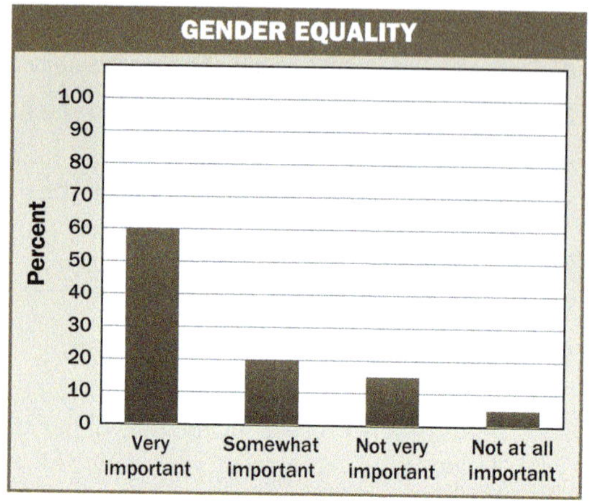

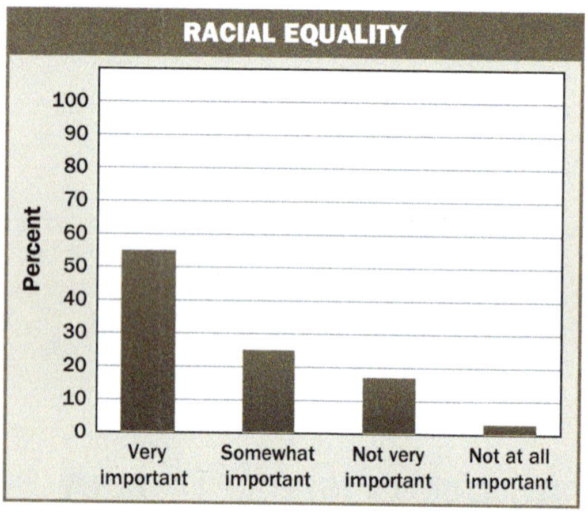

B. Conduct a survey in class or online with 10 friends regarding their beliefs on the most critical civil rights. Make bar graphs illustrating their responses. Present the results to your classmates.

Go to MyEnglishLab to listen again and answer critical thinking questions.

THINKING ABOUT LANGUAGE

Listen to the excerpts from the lecture and paraphrase each statement.

1. ....

2. ....

3. ....

4. ....

GROUP PRESENTATION

A. Read and discuss the question with one or more students.

Social movements have brought great change to countries all over the world. What other social movements do you know that have brought great change?

B. You will work with a small group to present a social movement that has brought great change to a culture or country. First, share stories on social movements. Then, select one movement and research details about it. Consider issues of organizational support, mobilization, and social injustice when creating your presentation.

1. What is the social movement your group will research?
2. What are some details on the movement that will illustrate your key points?

As you prepare, remember to paraphrase and elaborate on details to help your classmates understand key ideas.

C. Listen to each presentation.

Take notes and discuss the similarities and differences among all social movements presented.

Go to MyEnglishLab to listen to Professor Greenberg and to complete a self-assessment.

PART 2

Critical Thinking Skills

THE HUMAN EXPERIENCE
Sociology
FACTS AND OPINIONS 18

Part 2 moves from skill building to application of the skills that require critical thinking. Practice activities tied to specific learning outcomes in each unit require a deeper level of understanding of the academic content.

SOCIOLOGY

Facts and Opinions

UNIT PROFILE

In this unit, you will learn about social movements that have created change, such as the Black Freedom Movement. You will further investigate how activism emerges and social justice organizations are formed.

You will prepare a group presentation on what changes need to be made at your school or in your community.

OUTCOMES

- Identify facts through verbal and nonverbal signposts
- Identify opinions through verbal and nonverbal signposts
- Recognize facts and opinions in texts
- Interpret and utilize hedging devices

GETTING STARTED

Go to MyEnglishLab to listen to Professor Greenberg and to complete a self-assessment.

Discuss these questions with a partner or group.

1. What does the expression "together we stand, divided we fall" mean to you? Do you think this saying is always true? Can you think of any situations in your family or in society that illustrate your beliefs about this saying?
2. Why do you think people protest? Have you or has anyone you know ever participated in a protest? What was the outcome?
3. In the introduction, the speaker says that there were "multiple grassroots campaigns that happened during the time when Dr. King was most active." What are grassroots campaigns? Can you give some examples of grassroots campaigns during Dr. King's time and today?

CRITICAL THINKING SKILL

DISTINGUISHING FACTS FROM OPINIONS

WHY IT'S USEFUL By understanding how to distinguish a fact from an opinion, you can determine what can be proven through evidence and what cannot be proven. Using verbal and nonverbal signposts for facts and opinions in your own speeches or presentations will help your listeners recognize which statements are your beliefs and which statements you can support with evidence.

An important aspect of academic listening is **distinguishing a fact from an opinion**. This critical awareness can help you make the distinction between what can be proven and what may lack evidence. Many times making this distinction is very clear, while other times it is not as clear.

Facts are true statements that can be proven, or have objective evidence. Dates, percentages, and other numeric measurements are easily verified and are considered objective. Signposting factual statements with verbal cues is another indicator that the information is true and can be verified.

Opinions are statements of belief, judgment, or observation. While many people may have the same belief, that does not make it a fact. Similar to facts, opinions are easily distinguishable with signposts such as *I believe* or *I think*. However, speakers occasionally present certain information as factual, when it is not. In these cases, it is nearly impossible to distinguish it from fact without verifying the information through source-checking.

Facts and opinions are both necessary in academic discussions. Voicing opinions and using facts to support opinions are key elements for your academic success.

Go to MyEnglishLab to complete a vocabulary exercise.

NOTICING ACTIVITY

Listen to the lecture on activism and the relative deprivation theory. As you listen, notice what facts the speaker gives. How do you know they are facts? Share your ideas with a partner.

Go to MyEnglishLab to complete a skill practice and join in collaborative activities.

CULTURE NOTE

Marching for a Cause *Activism has a long history in North America. Even early settlers protested against unjust laws and regulations. One common form of protest is a march. This is when citizens gather and march in the streets, blocking traffic, in an area that decision makers, such as lawmakers, would be able to see or hear them. Marches were quite popular during Dr. King's time; however, they have been used in support of a vast array of causes, such as voicing opposition to wars or to lack of rights for women.*

SUPPORTING SKILL 1

IDENTIFYING FACTS THROUGH VERBAL AND NONVERBAL SIGNPOSTS

WHY IT'S USEFUL By recognizing verbal and nonverbal fact signaling, you can identify measurable, verifiable information. By using verbal fact signaling in your own presentations, you can make a stronger case to your audience, indicating which statements are verifiable.

Lecturers include both facts and opinions in their lectures. Facts are objective; they exist independently of anyone's perception or emotion. Identifying facts in spoken discourse can often be complicated. Unlike textbooks or other written material, you cannot "see" the source. There is no citation. However, speakers often use both verbal and nonverbal cues, or signposts, to indicate something is a fact.

USING VERBAL SIGNPOSTS

The language the speaker uses can help you determine whether the information is factual. When the speaker states a citation from a reliable source or mentions how the information is reliable, it is a fact. In addition, the *kind* of information given can distinguish it from an opinion. Numeric evidence is one type of information that can easily be used as evidence.

Language That Signposts a Fact	Information Given
According to Morrison, there are three keys to the relative deprivation theory.	**Sixty-four percent** of the American population felt bus segregation was unjust at the time of the Montgomery bus boycott.
Based on research conducted at Princeton, social movement organizations need charismatic leaders.	**In 1909**, the NAACP was formed in Illinois.
Well-known sociologists and historians determined that a single act of defiance brought light to the civil rights movement.	**Four in ten** African Americans report that they have been a victim of discrimination.
The government found the bus segregation unconstitutional.	Dr. King spoke out against unfair labor rights and the Vietnam War **at the Southern Christian Leadership Conference.**
As learned by past investigation, it was not Rosa Parks' intention to participate in an act of civil disobedience that day.	Dr. King visited the White House to campaign for voter rights **in the mid-1960s.**

Having a verbal signpost is not the only determiner of a fact. A fact is something that can be measured or validated. When in class, ask yourself if you can make a contrasting argument. If you can, it is most likely not a fact.

Examples

Opinion: Social movement organizations work because they bring about change.

Contrasting argument: Social movement organizations don't always work. Look at PETA (People for the Ethical Treatment of Animals). They are against killing animals and using their coats/skins for clothing. Yet, clothing made from animals, coats/skins is still manufactured today.

Fact: People involved in a social movement organization have a common goal.

Contrasting argument: This is a fact. A contrasting argument cannot be formed.

PART 2

USING NONVERBAL SIGNPOSTS

The language the speaker uses is one cue that the information you are hearing is a fact. The way the information is stated is a different type of cue, or signpost. It is a nonverbal signpost. Facts are generally spoken with a basic intonation pattern. The basic intonation pattern is a "step up, walk down" pattern. While your professor might use his or her voice to stress a key idea, it isn't an emphatic stress. Syllables other than the focal stress are of equal length. The vocal pattern, if diagrammed on paper, looks like this:

-i-
vis-
King -ted
-tor the
Doc- White
House.

Listen. When you hear this "step up, walk down" pattern, you can assume that the information stated is most likely a fact.

EXERCISE 1

Go to MyEnglishLab to complete a vocabulary exercise.

A. **Are you familiar with any organizations that have been formed to make a change? What are they? List some facts about these organizations.**

B. **Share your facts with a classmate. Use signposts when stating your facts. Was the information new to your classmate?**

C. **One well-known organization in the United States is the National Association for the Advancement of Colored People (NAACP). Work with one or two partners and share any facts you may know about this organization.**

D. Listen to this lecture about how the NAACP got its start. Which of these facts are given? For each fact identify the signpost that helped you determine it was a fact.

Fact	Verbal signpost	Nonverbal signpost
1. After the Civil War many politicians favored segregation.	....	....
2. After the war, politicians passed laws restricting the rights of African Americans.	....	....
3. African Americans who wanted to vote had to pay taxes, or take a test.	....	....
4. Organizations were formed to create more just laws.	....	....
5. Dubois led the Niagara Movement in 1905.	....	....
6. African Americans should work hard and avoid confrontation.	....	....
7. A violent race riot occurred in Springfield, Illinois.	....	....
8. NAACP is the most important advocate for African Americans.	....	....

Go to MyEnglishLab to complete a skill practice and join in collaborative activities.

SUPPORTING SKILL 2

IDENTIFYING OPINIONS THROUGH VERBAL AND NONVERBAL SIGNPOSTS

WHY IT'S USEFUL By recognizing verbal and nonverbal signposts of opinions, you can identify overgeneralizations, statements of bias, subjective statements, or statements that are observable but not measurable. By signposting your own opinions, you can make clear which statements are your beliefs, and you will be considered a more credible speaker.

Lecturers interject observations or opinions in their lectures. These are valuable and serve a purpose. Presentations often begin with an opinion and then are supported by facts. Determining which statements are opinions is not always straightforward. While some opinions may begin with "*I believe,*" "*In my opinion,*" or "*I think,*" that is not always the case in academic settings. Like facts, speakers often use both verbal and nonverbal cues—signposts—to indicate something is an opinion.

IDENTIFYING VERBAL SIGNPOSTS

There are three main types of verbal signposts to help you identify opinions. They are

- expressions used to introduce a personal opinion
- value and judgment words
- overgeneralizations

Value words can't be measured, and, when used in a statement, they can be debated easily. For example, "Social movement organizations are *useless*." While one person may believe this to be true, there are others who do not. It is debatable.

Judgment words are similar. They express what the speaker feels the outcome should be. For example, "By 2026, the government *must* ensure that all races have equal rights." The use of the modal *must* expresses a potential future outcome, rather than a proven fact.

Overgeneralizations are statements that are more general than can be proven. For example, "SMO leaders are *always* charismatic." These statements are subjective, or biased. Subjective and biased statements are influenced by personal opinions and can potentially be unfair.

Introducing a Personal Opinion	Value and Judgment Words	Overgeneralizing Words
I believe …	good	always
I bet / I'd bet …	ideal	anything
I imagine …	perfect	everything
I suspect …	bad	never
I think I'd say …	irrelevant	nothing
I think …	ordinary	
I'm sure …	outrageous	
Personally …	unnecessary	
	useless	

IDENTIFYING NONVERBAL SIGNPOSTS

Lecturers often use their voices to indicate an opinion. Strong opinions are said more emphatically, or with a stronger voice. The signposting words are generally said at a higher pitch and lengthened.

SMO lea ders are AL WAYS char is ma tic.

Listen. Emphatic, high-pitched statements like this one are a clue that what you are hearing is an opinion, rather than a fact.

EXERCISE 2

Go to **MyEnglishLab** to complete a vocabulary exercise.

A. Listen to two students studying Dr. King's reactions to various threats and violence. What opinions do the students have? Make notes about which statements are opinions.

B. Share your ideas with a classmate. Did you both agree on which statements were options?

C. Listen again. Decide whether each statement is an opinion or a fact. If it is an opinion, explain how you determined that.

1. Dr. King must have been furious that his home was bombed.

   □ Fact □ Opinion ....

2. Dr. King's speech after the bombing was not an easy speech to give.

   □ Fact □ Opinion ....

3. In his speech, Dr. King encouraged the continuation of peaceful actions.

   □ Fact □ Opinion ....

4. Dr. King knew that his home was wiretapped.

   □ Fact □ Opinion ....

5. Everyone should have a sit-down with the President.

   □ Fact □ Opinion ....

6. There was a backlash after the FBI authorized the wiretap on King's phone.

   □ Fact □ Opinion ....

> **CULTURE NOTE**
>
> ***John F. Kennedy*** *sometimes called JFK, was the 35th President of the United States. He was assassinated while still in office in 1963. JFK came from a family that is often considered American royalty. His brothers were also involved in politics. His brother Robert Kennedy was the attorney general, and it was he who persuaded the president to place secret listening devices in Dr. King's home.*

D. Check your answers with a classmate. Did you both find the same information?

Go to **MyEnglishLab** to complete a skill practice and join in collaborative activities.

INTEGRATED SKILLS

DISTINGUISHING BETWEEN FACTS AND OPINIONS IN TEXTS

WHY IT'S USEFUL By recognizing facts and opinions in written materials, you can critically analyze whether the information can be supported through evidence or whether it is the opinion of the writer.

Speakers often signal their ideas with signposts such as expressions of belief, judgment words, or terms of overgeneralizations. Like speakers, authors combine facts and opinions in writing. Reading critically allows you to better differentiate facts from opinions. The distinction is not always clear in text, as many authors avoid using the personal pronoun *I*. In addition, different types of written material lend themselves more to fact-giving, while others lend themselves more to opinion-giving. Newspaper and magazine articles tend to offer more opinion than fact. Textbook and journal articles tend to be more grounded in fact. These types of sources use citations to signal to the reader that the ideas are supported by evidence. A citation is one clear sign of a fact. Overall, textbooks tend to be more objective, while lecturers lean toward being more subjective. Although lecturers present facts, they often signal their agreement or disagreement with the information. These charts highlight the critical characteristics of fact- and opinion-giving in lectures and in printed materials.

SIGNALING FACTS	
Lecturers	**Academic Printed Materials**
• use signposts such as ***According to …*** • use numeric or other easily proven signposts such as ***In 1964 …***	• include the name of the source • offer numeric details • provide citations

SIGNALING OPINIONS	
Lecturers	**Academic Printed Materials**
• use signposts such as a personal expression of belief, a judgment term, or an overgeneralization • encourage agreement or disagreement and opinion-giving	• use an immeasurable adjective such as ***good*** or ***interesting*** or a verb of emotion, such as ***worry*** • use hedging devices

EXERCISE 3

A. With a partner, discuss nonviolent social movements and radical social movements. What are some characteristics of each? List your ideas.

Nonviolent Social Movements	Radical Social Movements
....	....
....	....
....	....
....	....

B. Read the textbook excerpt. As you read, pay attention to the signals used for facts and opinions.

Class Solidarity or Radical Separatism?

An Overview of Perspectives on Consciousness Raising in the African American Civil Rights Movement

Is racial equality best achieved through hard work and quiet struggle within a socio-political environment or by building a new, separate society unfettered by oppressive ideology? In the centuries-long struggle for equal rights, it seems that African American philosophers, activists, and citizens have approached the quest for equality in numerous ways, with each viewpoint offering new perspectives to the community as a whole. As far back as the early 19th century, some abolitionists and freedmen argued in favor of separatism—completely removing African Americans as a people from the direct control of the United States government (Walter 22). The nation of Liberia was formed by former North American and Caribbean slaves seeking to establish a new, sovereign nation. Decades later, faced with the violence and oppression of the Jim Crow era, figures like Marcus Garvey would try to persuade black citizens in North America to join the "back to Africa" movement, borne of the idea that true freedom from oppression could be found in their ancestral homeland.

During the civil rights era, the Black Nationalist and Black Separatist movements advocated not just for solidarity but also for a form of self-reliance that more moderate civil rights advocates found to be extreme (Kendall 21, 76). Moderate advocates, such as Dr. Martin Luther King Jr., worried that the positions of radical activists would harm the perception of the civil rights movement on the national level. For example, certain militant groups advocated in favor of armed self-defense organizations as a way to protect African Americans from violent hate groups like the Ku Klux Klan. Moderates were concerned that even raising the possibility of armed self-defense would likely inflame white racist hate groups and segregationist politicians, providing them the justification needed to enact stricter legislation.

According to meeting minutes, black radicals argued that the moderates' perspective was based in false consciousness and ended up supporting, not challenging, the ideology of an oppressive government that cared little about the safety or welfare of African Americans. Malcolm X, in his famous "The Bullet or The Ballot" speech, seemed to indicate that segregation was still in common practice by state and local governments despite being clearly and obviously illegal according to the Supreme Court. What, asked the radicals, did African Americans expect to gain from a government that could not even enforce its own laws?

In truth, despite the differing perspectives and often bitter arguments among the two sides, both groups were dedicated to raising the class consciousness of African Americans. Both groups found the ideology of American society oppressive and saw the harm done to African Americans as a serious problem. The primary difference between the two groups was simply the means by which they hoped to change society. Both were dedicated to consciousness-raising, but each group had a different understanding of what that entailed.

C. List four facts from the excerpt in one column and four opinions in the other column.

Facts	Opinions

D. Check your answers with a partner. Discuss what helped you identify opinions within the text.

CULTURE NOTE

The Black Panthers *One of the more radical social and political organizations that formed in response to racial and social unrest in the 1960s was the Black Panther Party, commonly known as the Black Panthers, or BPP. The Black Panthers originated in Oakland, California in 1966. The Black Panthers were known for their practice of militant self-defense, such as carrying guns in their communities on patrols to "police the police" (monitor and challenge police brutality). Their beliefs were connected to those of Lenin and Mao Tse Dong, who believed in "armed struggle" to achieve social change rather than nonviolent resistance. They called for violent revolution. In addition to their beliefs in violence, the Black Panthers also began several social programs in African American areas to promote self-reliance. These programs included health clinics for those with little or no medical care and a free breakfast program for children. Because of leadership conflicts, membership began to decline, and after 1972, the BPP was no longer active in the United States. Their organization was very controversial; many found their beliefs and methods too extreme to be effective.*

E. Work in groups of four. Two members of the group consider the benefits of nonviolent movements. Two members of the group consider the benefits of radical movements. Have an informal debate regarding which movement is more effective in creating change.

Benefits of Nonviolent Movements	Benefits of Radical Movements

Go to MyEnglishLab to complete a skill practice.

LANGUAGE SKILLS

INTERPRETING AND UTILIZING HEDGING DEVICES

WHY IT'S USEFUL By identifying hedging devices in presentations and lectures, you can differentiate facts from opinions more easily and determine a speaker's certainty about his or her statement. Incorporating hedging devices into your own speaking allows you to cautiously communicate your assertion.

During class lectures, presentations, and discussions, students often assert their ideas or claims. While a claim is an opinion, it is usually supported with facts. **Hedging** is a strategy used to cautiously express your assertion or opinion. Listeners are able to ascertain your level of certainty with the hedging device you use. A fact has 100 percent certainty, while an opinion has less than 100 percent certainty. The hedging device you choose shows how close to certain, or how uncertain, you are. There are several types of hedging devices. These are shown in the chart.

Device	Example	Explanation
Modal auxiliary verbs can, could, may, might, must, should	Great leaders can be a catalyst for change. The legislative changes of the 1960s **might** not have occurred had it not been for leaders like Dr. King.	Using a modal softens your opinion and expresses cautiousness to the listener. Listeners understand you are not 100% certain when you insert a modal. If the *can* is removed from the first example, it sounds like a fact. It is a very strong assertion.
Adverbs of approximation (modal adverbs) apparently, likely, perhaps, possibly, presumably, probably, arguably	The relative deprivation theory is **possibly** an explanation for the large number of SMOs during the 1960s and 1970s.	Like modal auxiliary verbs, modal adverbs communicate that you are not 100% certain.
Distancing verbs appear, indicate, look like, seem, suggest, tend	The theory **seems** to indicate that the characteristics of leaders are necessary for mobilization. Research in this area **suggests** that the organization must collectively agree on the message they wish to convey.	These statements often appear to be facts; however, the use of the distancing verb communicates that this is one's opinion. The speaker is cautiously and politely offering an informed opinion.
Compound hedges seems reasonable, seems / looks probable / likely / unlikely	It **seems reasonable** to conclude that sociologists have thoroughly examined this topic. It **looks likely** that other grassroots organizations will follow in their footsteps.	Compound hedges generally include an introductory verb and adverb of approximation. Using compound hedges communicates to your listeners why you have this opinion while at the same time remaining open to debate or argument.
Informal vagueness indicators and coordination tags Kind of, sort of And / or + everything, so, something, such, stuff, thing	Those sit-ins were **kind of** effective. The college students involved in those sit-ins spent numerous hours **or so**.	Like other hedging devices, these informal devices indicate a speaker's imprecision or approximation. These are commonly heard in small group discussions, but they are not often used in formal lectures or presentations.

EXERCISE 4

Rewrite each statement using the hedging device indicated.

1. The Southern Christian Leadership Conference made great strides in communicating the message of nonviolent protest. (distancing verb)

   ....

2. The Poor People's campaign orchestrated the massive march on the capital in Washington, D.C. (adverb of approximation)

   ....

3. The gradual rise of the African American influence mobilized the movement. (compound hedge)

   ....

4. The NAACP pushed for economic and political reforms. (informal vagueness indicator)

   ....

5. The Montgomery bus boycott signaled a change within the movement. (modal auxiliary verb)

   ....

6. Freedom rides and freedom songs promoted racial solidarity. (distancing verb)

   ....

EXERCISE 5

A. Listen to the lecture excerpt and take notes.

B. Use your notes to share what you heard with a classmate. Use hedging devices for those points that you are not certain of. Listen to your partner's ideas. How certain were you both?

Go to MyEnglishLab to complete a skill practice.

SUPPORTING SKILL 3

RECOGNIZING AND INTERPRETING STATEMENTS OF OPINION

WHY IT'S USEFUL Some statements that appear to be factual may contain elements of opinion as well. By identifying the kinds of language that often accompany statements of opinion, you will be able to recognize when an author is presenting a personal idea or position.

An **opinion** is defined simply as a person's "ideas or beliefs about a particular subject."

Fact:	As of 2014, the rate of union membership had fallen 9 percent over the past 30 years.
Fact + opinion:	It's a shame that as of 2014, the rate of union membership had fallen 9 percent over the past 30 years.

The former is a pure fact because the statement is wholly neutral, containing no language that suggests an opinion provided by the author. The latter is demonstrative of a fact framed by an opinion, signaled by the phrase *It's a shame that …*, which carries a connotation—one of the several types of language attributes to look for when attempting to recognize opinions within a text.

FEATURES OF STATEMENTS OF OPINION

- **Connotation** is a feeling or an idea that a word evokes beyond its literal meaning. Words may carry positive or negative connotations. Examples of words with positive connotations—words that indicate a favorable attitude—are *easygoing, youthful,* and *confident*. Examples of words with negative connotations include *uptight, immature,* and *arrogant*.
- **Tone** is the general feeling or attitude expressed in a piece of writing conveyed through elements such as word choice, selective use of examples and evidence, syntax, and punctuation. Categories of tone include humorous, approving, disapproving, persuasive, objective, informative, and formal. Study these two examples of tone:

Approving:	It was vitally important for the many who supported equality during the US civil rights movement to openly express their views in order to avoid disaster.
Informative:	The many who supported equality during the US civil rights movement openly expressed their views.

  The first sentence approves of the movement through its use of strong language: *vitally important, avoid disaster.* The second sentence simply informs, without employing any emphatic language. By accurately identifying tone, you are better equipped to determine a writer's goal.
- **Bias** refers to a writer's partiality toward a particular perspective. The writer may either be *biased toward* a viewpoint (showing support or positive feelings toward it) or *biased against* a viewpoint (demonstrating opposition or negative feelings toward it). An example of bias is the attitude of a proud parent toward his or her child. The parent may be so biased that he or she considers the child highly gifted even when, in fact, the child's abilities are not extraordinary. Sometimes bias in a text may be very clear upon first read; however, bias is often concealed and only uncovered after a deeper reading.

In the following example, the writer demonstrates a very negative attitude toward the Ku Klux Klan. Notice the negative bias conveyed in the underlined words and phrases. For the words *values* and *ideal*, the negativity is communicated by the quotation marks, turning otherwise positive words into sarcastic remarks.

> The Ku Klux Klan—a despicable organization that upholds "values" of white supremacy and anti-immigration—should be condemned by all individuals who believe in equality. While this group claims to promote American and Christian values, it actually has used terroristic methods to instill fear in and commit violence against those it deemed "impure." It has gone about this in inhumane and often brutal ways, including burning crosses, beating and maiming people who don't fit in with its "ideal" society, and even going so far as to murder them. Despite what its members argue, there is nothing positive or redeeming about this wretched organization.

- **Signal phrases** are another feature of some statements of opinion. A signal phrase may indicate the author's own opinion, or it may indicate the opinion of someone else.

Author's opinion:	In my opinion, the current administration seems to be putting civil rights on the back burner.
Opinion reported by an author:	The current administration is thought to be putting civil rights on the back burner.

The mere addition of the phrase *is thought to be* in the second example tells a reader that the writer is not expressing his or her own opinion; rather, the writer is conveying an opinion held by others.

Examples of Phrases Used to Signal an Opinion	
According to X	**According to** Mahatma Gandhi, there is no better tactic for achieving goals than civil disobedience; however, many disagree.
Apparently	There was **apparently** a lot of media support for civil rights leaders, but not enough support across the population as a whole.
From my perspective	**From my perspective**, racial integration is something that still has not been achieved in US society.
In my experience	**In my experience**, protesters genuinely strive to make their desires known without resorting to violence.
In my opinion	**In my opinion**, civil disobedience is a tactic that more groups calling for change should use.
In my view	**In my view**, people do not truly support equal rights if they only state it; it must be evident through their actions.
It is the opinion of X that	**It is the opinion of** many **that** the Voting Rights Act of 1965 was only one step toward ridding American society of racism.
It is thought that	**It is thought that** the politician George Wallace was incredibly racist; however, those who supported him contest this and maintain that he fought for what he thought was right.
It may be that	**It may be that** certain high-level politicians during the civil rights movement never supported equal rights for all.
X is considered	Henry David Thoreau **is considered** to be one of the first activists in the United States to publicly advocate civil disobedience.
X suggest(s) / state(s)	Many **suggest** that it is irresponsible to intentionally violate laws in acts of civil disobedience, but others strongly endorse such actions.

- **Source and author purpose** are two other features to consider when deciding if a statement is an opinion. The information within a textbook, or in a newspaper or magazine news report, for example, is meant to inform, typically in an unbiased manner. On the other hand, the objective of blog posts, editorials, and feature articles tends to be to persuade, meaning that the information found in them is much more likely to include opinions.

EXERCISE 1

A. Circle the word in each pair that has the more negative connotation.

1. oppressive / tyrannical
2. violate / disobey
3. discard / dump
4. mutinously / defiantly
5. introduce / impose
6. barbaric / inhumane

B. Read the passage. What is the tone? How does the author set that tone? Point to specific elements of the passage (e.g., word choice, selective use of examples and evidence, syntax, and punctuation) that helped you determine this.

Gandhi's Salt Strategy

Gandhi participating in the Salt March, 1930

1 Mahatma Gandhi's most successful acts of civil disobedience against Britain's oppressive rule aimed to involve people from all socioeconomic groups and bring sweeping changes to the entire society. These acts specifically employed methods of protest that were easily accessible to all. Regarded today as an exemplar of protest activism, Gandhi's so-called "khadi campaign" encouraged Indians to spin cotton into yarn, weave that yarn into cloth, and boycott British manufactured textiles. In a similar vein, Gandhi encouraged Indians to disobey British salt laws by producing their own salt. Spinning and weaving and salt-making are among the most humble of tasks, but according to Gandhi, they boosted self-respect among those viewed as the *hoi polloi*, they trained citizens to mobilize for a collective movement, and they provided people with constructive work that would eventually lead a nation to independence.

Khadi Campaign

2 Gandhi began his work as a civil rights leader not in India, but rather on the distant shores of South Africa, where he campaigned for equal rights for much of his two decades of residence there. Returning to his homeland of India in 1914 as a recognized rabble-rouser, he soon discarded Western clothing and donned the homespun cloth of India known as *khadi* as a way of symbolically casting off British rule. Britain controlled the textile market in India, and Gandhi began encouraging Indians to wear homespun cloth as a way of both

defying the British monopoly of the marketplace and increasing self-reliance. Traditional Indian clothing became not only a commodity, as it could be worn, but also a visual uniform of nationalism. The movement gained traction, and soon Gandhi's followers defiantly burned their British clothing and wore the traditional cloth.

Salt Campaign

3 The British imposed strict laws on the production and distribution of salt, which forced Indians to buy expensive, heavily taxed British salt. With meticulous care, Gandhi chose his method of protest against the British when he decided in 1930 to lead a 240-mile march to the sea to collect salt. His plan was met with disbelief when presented to the Indian authorities, but Gandhi defended his reasons, stating that salt was one of the most important necessities of life. He further called the tax inhumane and unjust, declaring that it was unconscionable to tax a commodity that millions of poor people required. Gandhi's idea, though initially met with skepticism, turned out to be ingenious because it created ripples that reached the farthest edges of the nation and spread word of the Indian independence movement throughout the world.

4 As with the khadi campaign, hundreds of thousands joined in Gandhi's Salt March. British-backed forces jailed more than 60,000 marchers and brutally beat many of them, but most marchers continued to adhere to nonviolent resistance even amidst the crackdown. The British eventually made concessions, and Gandhi's campaign gained a following abroad where his work was lauded, with *Time* magazine declaring him Man of the Year in 1930. Other civil rights leaders began to take notes for their own campaigns to come. India's victory came 17 years later in 1947, when the British succumbed to pressure and recognized India as an independent nation.

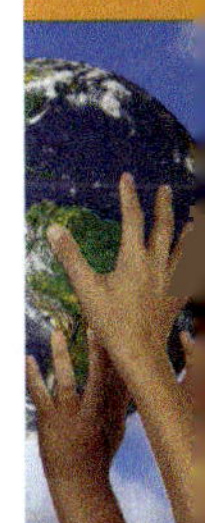

C. Read these excerpts from the passage, each of which contains biased language. Explain what language makes each excerpt biased.

1. Regarded today as an exemplar of protest activism, Gandhi's so-called "khadi campaign" encouraged Indians to spin cotton into yarn, weave that yarn into cloth, and boycott British manufactured textiles.
2. Spinning and weaving and salt-making are among the most humble of tasks, but according to Gandhi, they boosted self-respect among those viewed as the *hoi polloi*, they trained citizens to mobilize for a collective movement, and they provided people with constructive work that would eventually lead a nation to independence.
3. Returning to his homeland of India in 1914 as a recognized rabble-rouser, he soon discarded Western clothing and donned the homespun cloth of India known as *khadi* as a way of symbolically casting off British rule.
4. He further called the tax inhumane and unjust, declaring that it was unconscionable to tax a commodity that millions of poor people required.
5. Gandhi's idea, though initially met with skepticism, turned out to be ingenious because it created ripples that reached the farthest edges of the nation and spread word of the Indian independence movement throughout the world.
6. British-backed forces jailed more than 60,000 marchers and brutally beat many of them, but most marchers continued to adhere to nonviolent resistance even amidst the crackdown.

> **TIP**
>
> ***Biased or unbiased?*** *While it is true that news reports are intended to be informative (and thus unbiased), one part of them is often very biased: the quotes embedded in them. News reporters write their stories objectively, but the individuals who provide the quotes often give their opinions about the topic at hand.*

D. Discuss your answers with another student. Use information and examples from the passage to explain and support your answers.

SUPPORTING SKILL 4

RECOGNIZING AND INTERPRETING STATEMENTS OF FACT

WHY IT'S USEFUL By considering types of language that typically characterize facts, you will be able to evaluate whether a reading excerpt is indeed a fact (versus an opinion). This will further develop your critical thinking skills and your ability to analyze and interpret what you are reading.

A **fact** is a piece of information that is known to be true. The ability to identify a statement of fact, and to distinguish that statement of fact from other types of statements—statements of opinions and statements of facts + opinions—is essential to your understanding of a reading.

Features of Factual Statements

> **TIP**
>
> ***Be careful.*** *In academic writing, watch out for phrases like* researchers suggest, scholars lament, *and* historians have established. *At times, these phrases can be followed or preceded by pure facts, but they often contain a fact combined with the author's opinion about it. Facts are also frequently combined with opinions when an author reports on others' biases. Such an example of fact plus opinion is shown in this excerpt from the online reading "Distorting Effect":*
> However, in the years since his assassination in 1968, King's slow ascension to a hero's pedestal has, **scholars lament**, frozen his character in time, thereby watering down the way in which his message speaks to continuing racial inequality today.

- Phrases suggesting a citation, including:
  - According to
  - As reported by
  - As stated in
  - It is a fact that
  - The author discusses / explains / writes, etc.
  - The facts show that
  - The results demonstrate / indicate
- Direct and indirect quotes (which often include quotation marks and in-line citations)
- Neutrality of vocabulary: This refers to an absence of connotative language and bias as well as an objective tone.
- Hedging: This is a type of cautious language that is often used in academic writing when a writer is presenting facts and wants to be as precise as possible. Examples of hedging:
  - it appears
  - it could be the case that
  - may, might, can, could (modal verbs)
  - probable / possible
  - some
  - tend(s) (not) to
  - X indicate(s)
  - X suggest(s)
- Informative or enumerative tone: As mentioned earlier, an informative tone is one in which an author provides information about a topic without inserting any personal evaluation about the topic. When an author employs an enumerative tone, he or she is supplying a list of the objects, concepts, ideas, and so on that fall under a given construct, again, without adding opinions about the concept.

Informative: A large number of legislators, state representatives, and high-level government officials now believe in providing all individuals with equal opportunities.

Enumerative: Exactly 650 legislators, 401 state representatives, and 12 high-level government officials now believe in providing all individuals with equal opportunities.

However, the presence of an informative or enumerative tone does *not* mean that the information is necessarily purely factual. The inclusion of words that have strong connotations is often indicative of a statement of fact plus opinion. As mentioned earlier, authors sometimes interweave opinion with fact.

> Gandhi's Salt March was enormously influential, leading future civil rights leaders to adopt a tactic unparalleled by any other: civil disobedience.

While it is true that Gandhi's Salt March was influential, author bias is evident in the example above with the word "enormously." It is also a fact that future civil rights leaders adopted the tactic of civil disobedience, but it is clear that the author is inserting an opinion through the addition of the phrase "a tactic unparalleled by any other."

EXERCISE 2

A. Read this excerpt from "Gandhi's Influence" and identify the factual information. Circle the ten words and phrases in bold that are neutral. Then paraphrase five facts from the reading and write your paraphrases below.

> American civil rights movement **leader** Martin Luther King Jr. **drew heavily** upon the **strategies** of Mahatma Gandhi's campaign to combat **social injustice**, but he was not the first **civil rights leader** to draw parallels between the **oppression** of the Indian people and the injustice **inflicted upon** black people in America. In fact, King was one of many in **a long line** of leaders inspired by Gandhi's style of civil disobedience. **Decades** before King emulated Gandhi's **salt march** with his **historic march** from Selma to Montgomery, civil rights leaders were **working hard** to bring Gandhi's message **to the United States**. As early as the 1920s, **political leader** Marcus M. Garvey depended on Gandhi for intellectual legitimacy, and in 1929, **author and activist** W.E.B. Du Bois **published** a letter from Gandhi in an **influential NAACP magazine** that was widely distributed throughout **the black community**.

1. ....
2. ....
3. ....
4. ....
5. ....

B. Now read the full passage.

Gandhi's Influence

1 American civil rights movement leader Martin Luther King Jr. drew heavily upon the strategies of Mahatma Gandhi's campaign to combat social injustice, but he was not the first civil rights leader to draw parallels between the oppression of the Indian people and the injustice inflicted upon black people in America. In fact, King was one of many in a long line of leaders inspired by Gandhi's style of civil disobedience. Decades before King emulated Gandhi's Salt March with his historic march from Selma to Montgomery, civil rights leaders were working hard to bring Gandhi's message to the United States. As early as the 1920s, political leader Marcus M. Garvey depended on Gandhi for intellectual legitimacy, and in 1929, author and activist W.E.B. Du Bois

Continued

published a letter from Gandhi in an influential NAACP magazine that was widely distributed throughout the black community.

2 Gandhi's campaign targeted multiple social ills including the repressive rule of the British, the divisive "caste" system, and the pitting of Muslims against Hindus. It was Gandhi's focus on the integration of a group of people from the lowest caste, the "untouchables," that was of particular interest to many black Americans. Millions of Indians born into this caste system were marginalized and ostracized in Indian society to a degree that was almost unfathomable, and the integration Gandhi envisioned and labored for struck a chord with black Americans. In 1932, America's preeminent black newspaper, the *Atlanta Daily World*, printed a front-page article citing comments from Republican lawmaker William E. King about Gandhi's efforts to achieve integration for India's lowest class. The lawmaker compared the plight of the untouchables of India to Southern black people.

3 The message spread. In 1936, a group of leading black educators, including Howard Thurman, dean of historic Howard University, visited Gandhi in India. Gandhi asked the leaders why they had not yet adopted the approach of civil disobedience, stressing nonviolence as the only means for effective change. During and following World War II, many prominent leaders in the black community lauded Gandhi's work and prepared the way for an eventual charismatic leader of their own. Civil rights leader James Farmer studied Thurman's writings about Gandhi, and in 1942, he proposed a five-year plan of mobilization that called for acts of noncooperation and economic boycott, both of which constituted civil disobedience. Farmer went on to become director of the Congress of Racial Equality, an organization that led a series of acts of civil disobedience in protest against segregation on buses. Another leader in the black community, Howard University president Mordecai Wyatt Johnson, visited India in 1949 and returned inspired. When Martin Luther King Jr. attended seminary, he heard a sermon by Johnson about Gandhi and soon after bought six books about the Indian leader.

4 Johnson, Thurman, and others preached of Gandhi's greatness as a leader who followed revolutionary principles while adhering to nonviolent methods. Gandhi, who referred to the untouchable caste as "children of God," was echoed by King, who spoke of a moral obligation to uphold the values of all humans, especially the oppressed. King himself visited India in 1959 and later used many of Gandhi's strategies in the US civil rights movement.

C. Answer the questions.

1. Look back at Paragraph 2. Which information do you identify as facts? Why?

   ....

2. Reread this sentence from Paragraph 3. Identify the neutral verb(s) and the verb(s) with connotation: **Gandhi asked the leaders why they had not yet adopted the approach of civil disobedience, stressing nonviolence as the only means for effective change.**

   ....

3. Look back at Paragraph 4. Which sentence contains the most neutral language?

   ....

D. Discuss the questions in Part C with another student. Use information and examples from the passage to support your answers.

APPLY YOUR SKILLS

WHY IT'S USEFUL By applying the skills you have learned in this unit, you can successfully distinguish between facts and opinions in academic contexts. You can recognize which statements are supported by evidence and which statements show bias or reflect the speaker's perspective. By utilizing hedging language and by signposting facts and opinions in your own presentations, you can make a stronger argument in which it is clear to your listeners what your own views are.

ASSIGNMENT

Prepare a group presentation on a change that you would like to see made in your community or school. Use what you have learned on relative deprivation theory, social movement organizations, and activism to present your ideas.

BEFORE YOU LISTEN

A. Before you listen, discuss these questions with one or more students.

1. Considering historical events and cultural climates, what changes have resulted due to activism?
2. What makes a social movement organization effective in today's world?
3. What are the issues that surround social movement organizations today?

B. You will hear a lecture about a social movement called the Black Freedom Movement. This movement marked a change in how African Americans organized to fight segregation. As you listen, think about these questions.

1. What characterized the efforts of Dr. King and the NAACP to effect change?
2. How did later movements, such as the Black Freedom Movement, differ from earlier efforts?
3. What were the forces that brought about these changes?

C. Review the Unit Skills Summary. As you listen to the lecture and begin preparing your presentation, apply the skills you learned in this unit.

UNIT SKILLS SUMMARY

Identify facts.

- Listen for signposts.
- Pay close attention to voice.
- Recognize measurable evidence.

Identify opinions.

- Listen for signposts.
- Pay close attention to voice.
- Recognize judgment words and overgeneralizations.

Identify and utilize hedging devices such as:

- modal auxiliary verbs (*may, might*, etc.)
- adverbs of approximation (*apparently, probably*, etc.)
- distancing verbs (*appear, seem, tend*, etc.)
- compound hedges (*seems reasonable, looks likely*, etc.)
- indicators of vagueness and coordination tags (*kind of, and such*, etc.)

LISTEN

A. Listen to the lecture about the Black Freedom Movement. As you listen, take notes. Organize your notes according to verifiable fact versus the speaker's opinion.

B. Compare your notes with a partner. Did you both find the same facts and opinions? What listening skills from this unit can help you better identify fact versus opinion?

C. Work with a partner. Use your notes from the lecture to answer the questions from Before You Listen, Part B.

Go to MyEnglishLab to listen again and answer critical thinking questions.

THINKING CRITICALLY

Discuss these questions with another student.

1. Based on the lecture, what is the relationship between the Black Freedom Movement and Dr. King's early efforts?
2. What changes were made as a result of both movements? Based on what you heard, how did each movement play an important role toward bringing about these changes?
3. According to the speaker's conclusion, what led to further changes within these social movements? What do you think characterized the movements that followed?

THINKING VISUALLY

A. Look at this Venn diagram highlighting the similarities between social movements and collective behavior. Do you find any of these surprising? Why or why not? How does this diagram support what you heard in the lecture?

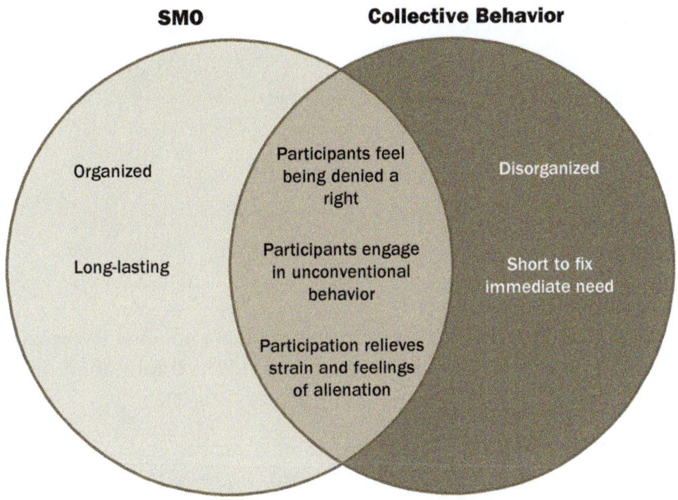

B. Conduct an online search on a current social movement organization. Investigate how the group began, their message, and the way in which they get their message across. Make a Venn diagram comparing it to either the Black Freedom Movement or Dr. King's civil rights movement. Present the diagram to your classmates and share your opinions about which group has been more effective.

THINKING ABOUT LANGUAGE

A. Listen to these excerpts from the lecture. After hearing each excerpt, rephrase the statement using a hedging device.

1. ....

2. ....

3. ....

B. Compare your answers with another student. Which hedging devices did you use? If you used different devices, how is your meaning different from your partner's?

GROUP PRESENTATION

A. Think about the lectures and other topics covered in this unit. Throughout history, people have organized themselves to make changes over a common issue, primarily over rights they felt they were being denied. Considering your current school and community, what issues need to have light shed upon them? Make a list.

B. Share your list with a small group. Prioritize your issues. Vote on which issue is most critical for the entire group.

1. With your group, create a message about this issue.
2. Develop your message, using evidence.
3. Use facts to support your group's opinions.
4. Determine the strategies you will employ to communicate your message.
5. Present your message and the strategies to your class.

C. Listen to each presentation.

As you listen, take notes. Determine what information is a fact and what information is an opinion. Consider the degree of certainty each group has in regards to the information they share.

D. Discuss these questions as a class.

Would you rally to support this group's cause? If not, what further evidence would they need to provide, or what strategies should they employ, to garner support?

Go to MyEnglishLab to listen to Professor Greenberg and to complete a self-assessment.

PART 3

Extended Lectures

THE HUMAN EXPERIENCE
Sociology
FIVE REVOLUTIONS 42

Part 3 presents authentic content written and delivered by university professors. Academically rigorous application and assessment activities allow for a synthesis of the skills developed in Parts 1 and 2.

SOCIOLOGY

Five Revolutions

UNIT PROFILE

In this unit you will watch a lecture entitled "Five Revolutions." This lecture examines the peaceful revolutionary work of Dr. Martin Luther King Jr. and evaluates events that have influenced social change movements throughout North American history.

You will research a grassroots movement that has impacted people's lives in a positive way and prepare a short presentation on the movement.

EXTENDED LECTURE

BEFORE YOU VIEW

Think about these questions before watching the lecture "Five Revolutions." Discuss them with another student.

1. What is a revolution?
2. Why do you think people revolt? What are some of the reasons people organize together to revolt?
3. Are you familiar with any 20th century revolutions? How have they impacted people's lives today?
4. Are there any revolutions happening now? What are they fighting for?

LECTURE

Go to MyEnglishLab to watch a lecture by Professor Jonathan Greenberg. Take notes while you listen. Then answer the questions in Check What You've Learned.

TIP

Taking notes *Three common methods for taking notes are outlining, the Cornell method, and charting or mapping. To learn more or to review these methods, refer to SOCIOLOGY Part 1.*

CHECK WHAT YOU'VE LEARNED

Think about the lecture you have just watched and refer to your notes. Answer each question.

1. In his introduction, Professor Greenberg refers to two revolutions. What are these revolutions and what connection do they have to one another?

2. What was Dr. King's purpose in referring to the story of Rip Van Winkle? Why does Professor Greenberg continue to refer to Rip Van Winkle?

3. Professor Greenberg mentions Dr. King's reference to a triple revolution. What are the other three revolutions the professor refers to? What are the similarities between those three revolutions and the two revolutions he mentions earlier?

4. What were the implications of the two questions Dr. King posed during his last sermon? What did he want people to understand?

5. What is Professor Greenberg referring to when he mentions the "moral force" of the Declaration of Independence? How does that force relate to the work of Dr. Martin Luther King Jr.?

6. What is meant by the term "rotten compromise and radical evil?" What rotten compromise does it refer to?

7. Can you identify Professor Greenberg's opinion regarding the Reconstruction period in relation to Civil Rights? What is it?

TIP

Identifying opinions *When listening to a lecture, you can identify the speaker's opinion through verbal and nonverbal signposts. For more on identifying opinions and on distinguishing opinions from facts, refer to SOCIOLOGY Part 2.*

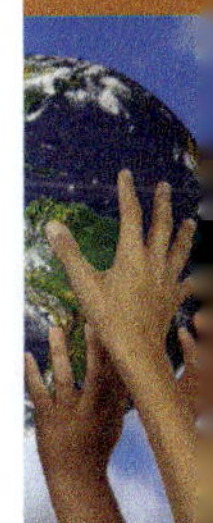

8. What are two things people in the 1950s and 1960s did to bring on the second revolution?

....

....

TIP

Paraphrasing *To clarify complex ideas, it can be helpful for speakers to paraphrase. This means that the speaker restates what was just said—a word, phrase, or idea—using different words. For more on paraphrasing, refer to SOCIOLOGY Part 1.*

9. Based on the lecture, what are Professor Greenberg's ideas regarding the *Brown vs. Board of Education* decision and its impact on segregation? Paraphrase them.

....

....

10. According to the lecture, how can you summarize our responsibilities as citizens?

....

....

THINKING CRITICALLY

Consider each situation in light of what you heard in the lecture. By yourself or with a partner, apply what you know about nonviolent protest movements to address each situation.

Situation 1 In his lecture, Professor Greenberg describes how nonviolent actions were pivotal acts of revolution. In the 1960s, nonviolence had an impact on problems of racism, poverty, and militarism. Choose one of these problems and describe how nonviolent protest can bring attention to the situation and create long-lasting change.

Situation 2 Science and technology have had an extraordinary impact on the course of human history over the last fifty 50 years. These advances, however, have not come without consequences. Improvements in science and technology have been linked to overpopulation, global food shortages, and radical climate change. The same technology that provides solutions is fraught with challenges. Using strategies from nonviolent protest movements, how could you design a campaign that would effectively address one of these challenges?

Go to MyEnglishLab to complete a critical thinking activity.

THINKING VISUALLY

A. Review the lecture, paying particular attention to important events and the years during which they occurred. Then create a timeline of 10 events mentioned by Professor Greenberg.

B. Compare your timeline with a partner. Follow these steps.

1. Take turns stating key events in your timeline.
2. When possible, explain how each event grew out of the previous event(s).
3. Work together and extend your timelines. Add key events from more recent years from international struggles for freedom and human rights.

THINKING ABOUT LANGUAGE

PARAPHRASING

Paraphrase the boldface words in the sentences.

1. The essential **trope**, ... of Dr. King's National Cathedral homily is the cautionary tale of Rip Van Winkle.
2. The American Revolution also harnessed a tremendous **moral force**. ....
3. Usually the party that suffers the cruelty and **humiliation**. ....
4. Throughout the South, African Americans were **coerced**, ..., into indentured servitude and forced labor by white plantation owners.
5. As a result, only a tiny **fraction**, ..., of African Americans in 1955 were registered to vote.
6. Dr. Martin Luther King Jr. spoke about a triple revolution **unfolding**, ..., in the present time.

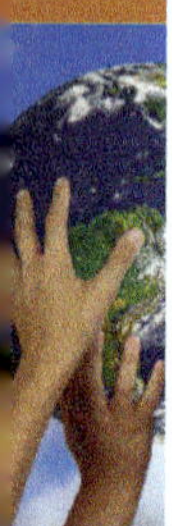

HEDGING

Rewrite each assertive statement using a hedging device.

> **TIP**
>
> ***Hedging devices*** *Speakers use hedging devices to soften, or, more cautiously, assert their opinion. For common hedging devices, see SOCIOLOGY Part 2.*

1. In life, too many people find themselves living amidst a great period of social change, and yet they fail to develop the new attitudes that the new situation demands.

   ....

   ....

2. The sole purpose of democratic government is to secure the rights of life, liberty, and the pursuit of happiness.

   ....

   ....

3. The compromise made to forge a unified nation, a more perfect union of all former American colonies north and south, was a rotten compromise.

   ....

   ....

4. The end of reconstruction effectively condemned African Americans in the former Confederacy to re-enslavement under new forms of coercion for decades to come.

   ....

   ....

5. Time after time Dr. Martin Luther King Jr. brought community and municipal struggles to the national media, thus triggering the pressure required to end local injustices.

   ....

   ....

6. Our responsibility as human beings is to join the powerful nonviolent struggle against racism, poverty, and militarism in the United States and throughout the world.

....

....

INDIVIDUAL PRESENTATION

The second revolution highlighted in the lecture began as a grassroots movement that spread across the country and the world to ignite a change. What are some other grassroots movements that have impacted people's lives? When and where did they begin? How did the message spread? How have people's lives been changed as a result?

Topic: Grassroots movement that has impacted people's lives in a positive way.

RESEARCH

A. Investigate other grassroots movements. Select a movement that interests you.

Grassroots movement..

B. Research your grassroots movement by seeking out primary sources. Check that the materials you use and cite are from reputable and respected publications.

C. Prepare your presentation. Be sure to present your main ideas clearly and to support your ideas with evidence.

D. Practice presenting to a partner.

E. While listening to your partner, ask him or her to elaborate on ideas where you would like more information.

> **TIP**
>
> ***Elaborating on ideas*** *To explore a topic in greater depth, it is important to ask the speaker for more details about a particular point in order to receive a deeper explanation. For more information on elaboration, refer to SOCIOLOGY Part 1.*

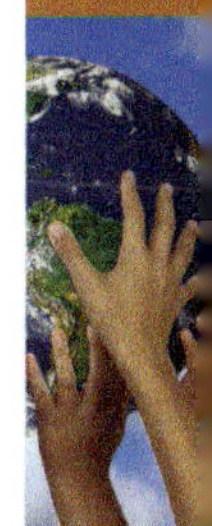

PRESENT

A. Listen to each class member's presentation. As you listen, complete the chart.

Movement	Time Period	Place	Key Leaders	Changes

B. After the presentations, have a class discussion on each movement. Be sure to utilize turn-taking techniques. Discuss how each movement has impacted people's lives. Which movements have impacted the greatest number of lives? Which movements have brought about the most critical changes?

Go to MyEnglishLab to complete a collaborative activity.

Credits

Front cover: DrAfter123/Getty Images; Part and unit openers (multi use): Budai Romeo Gabor/Fotolia (gold coins), Nik_Merkulov/Fotolia (leaf with water droplets), Scisetti Alfio/Fotolia (old letter), Vichly4thai/Fotolia (red molecule dna cell), Tobkatrina/123RF (children's hands holding earth); Page viii (top): Bettmann/Getty Images 514694602; viii (bottom): Ian Dagnall/Alamy Stock Photo; viii: Joe Gough/Shutterstock; ix: Everett Collection/Newscom; x (top): Skreidzeleu/Shutterstock; x (bottom): Brandon Bourdages/123RF; 2: Bettmann/Getty Images 514694602; 3: Ian Dagnall/Alamy Stock Photo; 5: Joe Gough/Shutterstock; 15 (top, right) Everett Historical/Shutterstock; 15 (bottom, right): Everett Historical/Shutterstock; 15 (top, left): Todd Bannor/Alamy Stock Photo; 15 (bottom left): AFP/Getty Images; 18: Everett Collection Inc/Alamy Stock Photo; 19: Pixel Embargo/Shutterstock; 22: Photos 12/Alamy Stock Photo; 30: Everett Collection/Newscom; 36: Bettmann/Getty Images; 38: Everett Collection/Newscom; 42: Brandon Bourdages/123RF; 44: Skreidzeleu/Shutterstock; 45: Boris15/Shutterstock.